Franz LISZT

HUNNENSCHLACHT

Symphonic Poem No. 11

S. 105

Study Score
Partitur

PETRUCCI LIBRARY PRESS

INTRODUCTION

The present score is a reissue of one from the Franz Liszt-Stiftung edition, originally published by Breitkopf & Härtel from 1907-1936. The edition was prepared in an effort to publish the entire oeuvre of Franz Liszt. Editors included such prominent musicians as Béla Bartok, Ferruccio Busoni, Eugène d'Albert and José Vianna da Motta – some of whom studied with Liszt – as well as scholars like Peter Raabe, who would later compile the first catalog of the composer's works. The need for a complete edition was already apparent by the time of Liszt's death. Although some of his piano music had regularly appeared in new editions throughout his life, these works were by no means representative of even his pianistic output. A far more unfortunate fate was left for his orchestral music - which would usually be issued only once, soon to go out of print and later scarcely available. The Liszt-Stiftung edition revived many works that had fallen into relative obscurity and was therefore handsomely welcomed.

The edition was sadly never completed. The publication activity was brought to a premature end by the time of the Second World War. All in all the incomplete edition encompassed 34 volumes, among others two symphonies, the symphonic poems, some concert works, a couple of piano arrangements and 11 volumes of original works for piano – a mere fraction of the composer's output – but the edition would nonetheless break the ground for Liszt research during the 20th century for a number of reasons. First, it brought to light a number of late pieces that would put Liszt as a forerunner of experimental music and firmly establish his position as such. Second, it revealed the diversity of Liszt's output, which up until that time had been best known as an important addition to the piano repertoire. Third, it displayed the complex and characteristic nature of many of his works by being the first edition to show and make use of several alternative (sometimes vastly different) versions and sources. Last but not least, it would provide the world with a generally reliable edition of easy availability and very high standard for its day.

The Bavarian State Library acquired a complete copy of said edition and decided to digitize it in 2008. By that time more than 70 years had passed since its publication, effectively rendering the edition out of copyright and free for any use. Each and every page was scanned and uploaded to their online digital collection. While this was a great effort in itself, the site has a rudimentary interface, is difficult to navigate and the scores are not in the context of relevant information. One of our users decided to also upload it to our site, the International Music Score Library Project (IMSLP) / Petrucci Music Library, the unique wiki-based repository of musical scores, composers and indexes that anyone can edit and amend. Through the effort of a single user, Mattias K. (piupianissimo), the entire edition is now easily available worldwide to those who wish to perform and study the composer's music in a historical context, since as the case is with Liszt's music, many early editions exist and many are readily available on the site and many more will be available in the future. IMSLP is as such a valuable resource available to the scholar but even more to the performer who is always a mere mouse click away from scores that have not been in print since the turn of the past century, or that are otherwise hard to come by. The availability, quantity of ease of access for online scores will soon exceed those of the traditional medium of print. Nevertheless new works have always been published through the printed medium and this tradition is going to persist for many years to come even if complemented by the digital medium. Of course an important fact to stress is that the availability of digital scores online does not exclude the need of printed score since neither one can replace the comfort and neatness of one another. The quality of a bound reprint or new engraving exceeds that of a score printed at home.

I discovered IMSLP back in early 2006 when it first began. At that time many scores were scattered on the net either privately or on commercial collection sites. Many of these sites had a considerably large collection but sadly many had restrictions on number of downloads per day and the process of contributing to them was riddled with bureaucracy. IMSLP was the first free site where anyone could contribute and upload any kind of musical scores. I have personally searched and uploaded many works – particularly those of Liszt – and the future of the site is nothing but bright. At the time of its start only a handful of scores were available on the site but through the effort of its users IMSLP has grown to be the largest collection of scores available on the Internet.

Hunnennschlacht is the eleventh work in a series of thirteen symphonic poems composed by Franz Liszt. It was composed from 1855-57 and first published in 1861 by Breitkopf und Härtel of Leipzig. The dedicatee is Princess Carolyne zu Sayn-Wittgenstein. This score is from the sixth volume of the Franz Liszt-Stiftung edition, edited by Otto Taubmann and published in 1910. The score, along with a number or arrangements, is also available directly at the following URL:

http:// imslp.org/wiki/Hunnenschlacht,_S.105_(Liszt,_Franz)

Soren Afshar (Funper)

Summer, 2011

COMPOSER'S PREFACE

Eine Aufführung, welche den Intentionen des Komponisten entsprechen und ihnen Klang, Farbe, Rhythmus und Leben verleihen soll, wird bei meinen Orchester-Werken am zweckmässigsten und mit dem geringsten Zeitverlust durch geteilte Vor-Proben gefördert werden. Demzufolge erlaube ich mir, die HH. Dirigenten, welche meine symphonischen Dichtungen aufzuführen beabsichtigen, zu ersuchen, der General-Probe Separat-Proben mit dem Streich-Quartett, andere mit Blas- und Schlag-Instrumenten vorangehen zu lassen.

Gleichzeitig sei mir gestattet zu bemerken, dass ich das mechanische, taktmässige, zerschnittene Auf- und Abspielen, wie es an manchen Orten noch üblich ist, möglichst beseitigt wünsche, und nur den periodischen Vortrag, mit dem Hervortreten der besonderen Accente und der Abrundung der melodischen und rhythmischen Nuanzierung, als sachgemäss anerkennen kann. In der geistigen Auffassung des Dirigenten liegt der Lebensnerv einer symphonischen Produktion, vorausgesetzt, dass im Orchester die geziemenden Mittel zu deren Verwirklichung sich vorfinden; andernfalls möchte es ratsamer erscheinen, sich nicht mit Werken zu befassen, welche keineswegs eine Alltags-Popularität beanspruchen.

Obschon ich bemüht war, durch genaue Anzeichnungen meine Intentionen zu verdeutlichen, so verhehle ich doch nicht, dass Manches, ja sogar das Wesentlichste, sich nicht zu Papier bringen lässt, und nur durch das künstlerische Vermögen, durch sympathisch schwungvolles Reproduzieren, sowohl des Dirigenten als der Aufführenden, zur durchgreifenden Wirkung gelangen kann. Dem Wohlwollen meiner Kunstgenossen sei es daher überlassen, das Meiste und Vorzüglichste an meinen Werken zu vollbringen.

Weimar, März 1856.

Pour obtenir un résultat d'exécution correspondant aux intentions de mes œuvres orchestrales, et leur donner le coloris, le rhythme, l'accent et la vie qu'elles réclament, il sera utile d'en préparer la répétition générale par des répétitions partielles des instruments à cordes, à vent, en cuivre, et à percussion. Par cette méthode de la division du travail on épargnera du temps en facilitant aux exécutants l'intelligence de l'ouvrage. Je me permets en conséquence de prier MM. les chefs d'orchestre qui seraient disposés à faire exécuter l'un de ces Poèmes symphoniques, de vouloir bien prendre le soin de faire précéder les répétitions générales, des répétitions préalables indiquées ci-dessus.

En même temps j'observerai que la mesure dans les œuvres de ce genre demande à être maniée avec plus de mesure, de souplesse, et d'intelligence des effets de coloris, de rhythme, et d'expression qu'il n'est encore d'usage dans beaucoup d'orchestres. Il ne suffit pas qu'une composition soit régulièrement bâtonnée et machinalement exécutée avec plus ou moins de correction pour que l'auteur ait à se louer de cette façon de propagation de son œuvre, et puisse y reconnaître une fidèle interprétation de sa pensée. Le nerf vital d'une belle exécution symphonique gît principalement dans la compréhension de l'œuvre reproduite, que le chef d'orchestre doit surtout posséder et communiquer, dans la manière de partager et d'accentuer les périodes, d'accuser les contrastes tout en ménageant les transitions de veiller tantôt à établir l'équilibre entre les divers instruments, tantôt à les faire ressortir soit isolément soit par groupes, car à tel moment il convient d'entonner ou de marquer simplement les notes, mais à d'autres il s'agit de phraser, de chanter, et même de déclamer. C'est au chef qu'il appartient d'indiquer à chacun des membres de l'orchestre la signification du rôle qu'il a à remplir.

Je me suis attaché à rendre mes intentions par rapport aux nuances, à l'accélération et au retard des mouvements, etc. aussi sensibles que possible par un emploi détaillé des signes et des expressions usitées; néanmoins ce serait une illusion de croire qu'on puisse fixer sur le papier ce qui fait la beauté et le caractère de l'exécution. Le talent et l'inspiration des artistes dirigeants et exécutants en ont seuls le secret, et la part de sympathie que ceux-ci voudront bien accorder à mes œuvres, seront pour elles le meilleur gage de succès.

Weimar, Mars 1856.

In order to secure a performance of my orchestral works which accords with their intentions, and which imparts to them the colour, rhythm, accent and life that they require, it is recommended that the general rehearsal should be preceded by separate rehearsals of the Strings, Wind, Brass, and instruments of percussion. By this division of labour time will be saved, and the executants will more rapidly be made familiar with what is required of them. I therefore venture to request that conductors, who are pleased to bring one or the other of my symphonic poems to a hearing will adopt the plan formulated above.

At the same time I may be allowed to remark that it is my wish that the mechanical, bar by bar, up and down beating of time, which obtains in so many places, should as far as possible be discarded, and that only the periodic divisions, with the prominence of certain accentuation and the rounding off of melodic and rhythmical nuances should alone be regarded as indispensable. The vitality of a symphonic performance depends upon the intellectual perception of the conductor, presuming that suitable material for its realisation is to be found in the orchestra; failing this it would seem to be advisable to hold aloof from works which do not claim a promise of every-day popularity.

Although I have endeavoured to make my intentions clear by providing exact marks of expression, I cannot conceal from myself that much, and that perhaps the most important, cannot be set forth on paper, but can only be successfully brought to light by the artistic capability and the sympathetic and enthusiastic reproduction by both conductor and executants. It may therefore be left to my colleagues in art to do the most and best that they can for my works.

Weimar, March 1856.

F. Liszt.

HUNNENSCHLACHT.

(Nach W. Kaulbach.)

SYMPHONISCHE DICHTUNG Nr.11 VON F. LISZT.

Wer kennt nicht Wilhelm v. Kaulbachs „Hunnenschlacht", eines seiner genialsten Gemälde, das erste, welches den Namen seines Schöpfers zur allgemeinen Berühmtheit erhob? Es befindet sich, als eines der sechs grossen Wandgemälde welthistorischen Inhaltes, im Treppenhause des Neuen Museums zu Berlin, und verewigt die gedankenreiche Sage von dem Kampfe zwischen den Geistern der gefallenen Hunnen und Christen vor den Toren Roms. Von der leichenbedeckten Walstatt erheben sich die Gespenster in gewaltig bewegten Gruppen zu den Wolken und setzen dort ihre Vernichtungsschlacht fort. Die Geisel Gottes, der blutige Attila, stürmt mit seinen wilden Horden noch einmal gegen die Römerscharen an, welche unter dem Zeichen des Kreuzes kämpfen und siegen. — Das Licht des Christentums zerstört die Finsternis des Heidentums.

Dies grossartige Motiv von gespensterhafter, dämonischer Natur gab Franz Liszt die Anregung zu seiner symphonischen Dichtung. — Im Beginn derselben wirbeln die Figuren der gedämpften Violinen wie Nebelwolken auf; sie verdichten sich mehr und mehr, je höher sie steigen; wir hören die Hörner-Schlachtrufe der Hunnen, welchen die Trompetensignale der Römer antworten. Mit einem wilden Schlachtgesang stürzen sich die gefallenen Hunnen in die Geisterschlacht; ein Choralgesang geleitet die kämpfenden Geister der Römer, welche dem wütenden Ansturm Trotz bieten. Immer fanatischer wogt der Vernichtungskampf, immer grimmiger wird das Gewühl — bis plötzlich Licht durch die finsteren Wolken blitzt: es geht vom siegenden Kreuze aus. Mächtige Fanfaren verkünden den Triumph des Christentums!

BATAILLE DES HUNS.

(D'après Kaulbach.)

POÈME SYMPHONIQUE No. 11 DE F. LISZT.

Kaulbach nous disait une fois comment, dans l'une des dernières conversations qu'il eut avant de quitter Rome avec un historien de ses amis, le jeune savant raconta la légende qui s'était attachée à la terrible bataille livrée dans les Champs Catalauniens (451) par Théodoric, à la tête des peuples chrétiens, à Attila, roi des Huns, chef de leurs hordes païennes, ajoutant que la lutte avait été si acharnée, au dire du chroniqueur qui narre le fait, qu'à peine les derniers rayons du jour furent-ils éteints, les survivants épouvantés crurent apercevoir, à travers les ombres de la nuit tombante, le combat se continuer entre les âmes des morts, toutes enflammées encore des rages et des fureurs qui les avaient animées peu d'instants auparavant.

Ce récit ne cessa de préoccuper la pensée du grand artiste; il s'en était emparé, il l'obsédait si bien, qu'en traversant peu après les champs de Trasimène, témoins d'un combat non moins long, non moins nombreux, non moins meurtrier, la légende du V° siècle prit tout d'un coup corps à ses yeux. — Dans les brouillards qui flottaient aux derniers reflets du couchant sur les eaux du lac, il distingua des figures, des groupes; ces combattants fantastiques se détachèrent toujours davantage, ils devinrent vivants à ses regards. Son tableau était fait. Mais, avec cette tendance philosophique qui marqua toujours à un noble coin les conceptions de son génie, Kaulbach vit en cette lutte suprême de Théodoric contre Attila, deux principes s'entrechoquer: la barbarie et la civilisation, le passé et l'avenir de l'humanité. Aussi, en mettant en présence ses deux héros, il éclaira l'un d'une lueur verdâtre, livide, cadavéreuse, comme un fait malfaisant, malgré la hauteur, l'audace, la puissance de volonté spontanée qui éclate dans toute sa personne; il enveloppa l'autre, plus concentré dans son attitude, plus calme, plus faible aussi comme individu — car il est supporté par ses alliés, Mérovée le Franc, Aëtius le Romain — d'une lumière solaire, féconde,

BATTLE OF THE HUNS.

(After Kaulbach.)

SYMPHONIC POEM No. 11 BY F. LISZT.

Kaulbach told me how, in one of the last conversations which he had before leaving Rome with an historian, who was one of his friends, the young savant related to him the legend of the terrible battle which in 451 Théodoric, at the head of his Christian people, waged against Attila, King of the Huns, and chief of their Pagan hordes, adding that the combat was so furious that in accordance with the chronicler's narration, hardly were the last rays of the sun extinguished when the frightened survivors believed that they beheld, as the shades of night descended upon them, the continuation of the combat between the souls of the slain, who were again inflamed by the rage and fury which had animated them but a moment before.

This story incessantly engrossed the attention of the great artist: it took such complete possession of him, that shortly afterwards, while traversing the fields of Trasimène, which had witnessed a combat not less long, on no less grand a scale, and not less murderous, the legend of the fifth century at once took full shape in his eyes. — In the mist which floated upon the surface of the lake during the last rays of the setting sun, he distinguished figures and groups; those fantastic combatants became more and more manifest till they became living in his sight. His picture was realized. But with that philosophic tendency which always raises the conception of his genius to a point of nobility, Kaulbach saw that in this supreme struggle of Théodoric with Attila two principles clashed with each other: barbarism and civilisation, the past and the future of huemanity. Therefore, in bringing his two heroes before us, he exhibited the one in a pale green, livid and cadaverous light, as if he were an evil being, in spite of the greatness, the boldness, the power of his spontaneous will, which environed his whole person; the other more concentrated in his attitude, more calm, more feeble also as an individual, — for he

Das Orchester schweigt: die Waffen senken sich. Wir hören Orgelklänge; sie intonieren den uralten Choral:

> Crux fidelis, inter omnes
> Arbor una nobilis,
> Nulla silva talem profert.
> Fronde, flore, germine
> Dulce lignum, dulce clavos,
> Dulce pondus sustinet.

Sanfte, flüsternde Stimmen ringen sich jetzt durch Nacht und Nebel empor: der Kampf ist aus; Frieden und Ruhe kehren in Roms Gefilde zurück. Der Schlachtgesang wird zum Dankgebet! In hoc signo vinces!

---

bienfaisante et envahissante, qui émane de la Croix dont il est précédé, comme d'un drapeau vainqueur.

La composition de cette fresque, acclamée comme un incontestable chef-d'œuvre du maître, est d'accord avec la vérité et la tradition historique, qui fit toujours d'Attila, surnommé le Fléau de Dieu, l'idéal de la barbarie féroce, tandis que le pape Léon-le-Grand, dont les supplications sauvèrent Rome de son invasion, les évêques Geminiani, Lupo, d'autres encore, qui rachetèrent d'autres villes d'une destruction certaine, demeuraient dans l'esprit des peuples la personnification des secours célestes qui protègent et assistent les nations chrétiennes.

En écoutant parler Kaulbach et en contemplant son œuvre merveilleuse que les générations admireront et étudieront, il nous sembla que sa pensée se laisserait transporter en musique, cet art pouvant reproduire l'impression des deux lumières surnaturelles et contrastantes, par deux motifs, dont l'un représente la furie des passions barbares qui poussaient les Huns à la dévastation de tant de pays, au carnage de tant de populations; dont l'autre porte en lui les forces sereines, les vertus irradiantes de l'idée chrétienne. Cette idée n'est-elle pas comme incarnée dans l'antique chant grégorien: Crux fidelis?

Le peintre crut voir surgir ses personnages dans les brumes d'un soir d'été; le musicien crut entendre, au sein de la mêlée sanglante, s'élever en un chœur formidable les cris des assaillants, le choc des armes, les rugissements des blessés, les imprécations des vaincus, les gémissements des mourants, pendant qu'il saisissait, venant d'un vague lointain, les accents d'une prière, d'un chant sacré, montant au ciel du fond des cloîtres, dont il emplissait seul le silence. Plus le tumulte de la bataille devenait assourdissant, plus ce chant grandissait en force et en puissance. Les deux thèmes se rapprochant toujours, finirent par se toucher, s'étreindre, lutter corps à corps, comme deux géants, jusqu'à ce que celui qui s'identifie avec le vrai divin, la charité universelle, le progrès dans l'humanité, l'espérance transmondaine, fût victorieux et répandit sur toutes choses son jour radieux, transfigurant, éternel!

(F. Liszt.)

---

was supported by his allies Mérovée the Frank, Aetius the Roman — he enveloped with a brilliant light, fruitful, beneficent and penetrating, which proceeded from the cross which was carried before him like a victorious banner.

The composition of this fresco, incontestably regarded as a chef-d'œuvre of this master, is in accordance with truth and historic tradition, which have always represented Attila, surnamed the Scourge of God, as the ideal of ferocious barbarism, while Pope Leo the Great, whose prayers saved Rome from his invasion, the Bishops Geminiani, Lupo, and others who rescued other towns from certain destruction, survived in the spirit of the people as the personification of the Celestial succour, which protects and helps Christian nations.

After listening to Kaulbach's talk, and contemplating his marvellous work, which will be admired and studied by generations to come, it seemed to me that his idea might suitably be transferred to music, and that this art was capable of reproducing the impression of the two supernatural and contrasting lights, by means of two motives, of which one should represent the fury of the barbarous passion, which drove the Huns to the devastation of so many countries and to the slaughter of so many people; while the other represents the serene powers, the virtues irradiating from Christianity — Is not this idea incarnated in the ancient Gregorian Hymn: Crux Fidelis?

The painter thought that he saw his personages arise from the mist of a summer eve; the musician thought that he heard in the midst of a sanguinary fight the cries of the combatants, the clash of arms, the wails of the wounded, the imprecations of the conquered, the groans of the dying, mingling in a terrible chorus, while at the same time as if coming from a distance he recognised the accents of a prayer, the sacred hymn, mounting to heaven from the depths of the cloister, whose silence it alone breaks. The more deafening the tumult of the battle became, the more this hymn increased in force and power. The two motives, gradually approaching each other, finish by uniting; pressing upon each other they contend in a hand-to-hand combat, like two giants, till the one which is identified with divine truth, universal charity, the progress of humanity, and a hope beyond the world, is victorious and sheds over all things a radiant, transfiguring, and eternal light.

After the 1854 relief by Ernst Rietschel

INSTRUMENTATION

2 Flutes

Piccolo

2 Oboes

2 Clarinets

2 Bassoons

4 Horns

3 Trumpets

3 Trombones

Tuba

Timpani

Cymbals

Organ

Violins I

Violins II

Violas

Violoncellos

Basses

Duration: ca. 16 minutes

First Performance: December 29, 1857
Weimar: Hofkapelle Weimar
Franz Liszt, conductor

ISBN: 978-1-60874-031-5

This score is an unabridged reprint of the score
first issued in Leipzig by Breitkopf & Härtel, 1910. Plate F.L. 11

Printed in the USA
First Printing: December, 2011

Hunnenschlacht

Symphonic Poem No. 11

S. 105

Franz Liszt (1811–1886)

Tempestoso, Allegro non troppo.

Kleine Flöte.

2 Flöten.

2 Hoboen.

2 Klarinetten in B.

2 Fagotte.

1.u.2. Horn in F.

3.u.4. Horn in F.

1.u.2. Trompete in C.

3. Trompete in C.

2 Tenorposaunen.

Bassposaune u. Tuba.

3 Pauken in As.C.G.

(mit Schwammschlägeln *with sponge-headed drumsticks* avec des baguettes d'éponge)

Becken.
(Ohne grosse Trommel.)
(senza cassa)

(mit Holzpaukenschlägeln *with wooden drumsticks* avec des baguettes de bois)

Orgel.

tacet bis Seite 57.

1. Violinen.

con sordini

2. Violinen.

NB. con sordini

Bratschen.

con sordini

Violoncelle.

con sordini

Kontrabässe.

Tempestoso, Allegro non troppo.

NB. Für den Dirigenten. Das ganze Kolorit soll anfangs sehr finster gehalten sein, und alle Instrumente müssen geisterhaft erklingen.
Note for the Conductor. The whole coloring must at first be very sombre and all the instruments like spectres in tone.
Pour les chefs. Tout le coloris au commencement doit rester sombre et tous les instruments doivent retentir d'une façon sinistre.

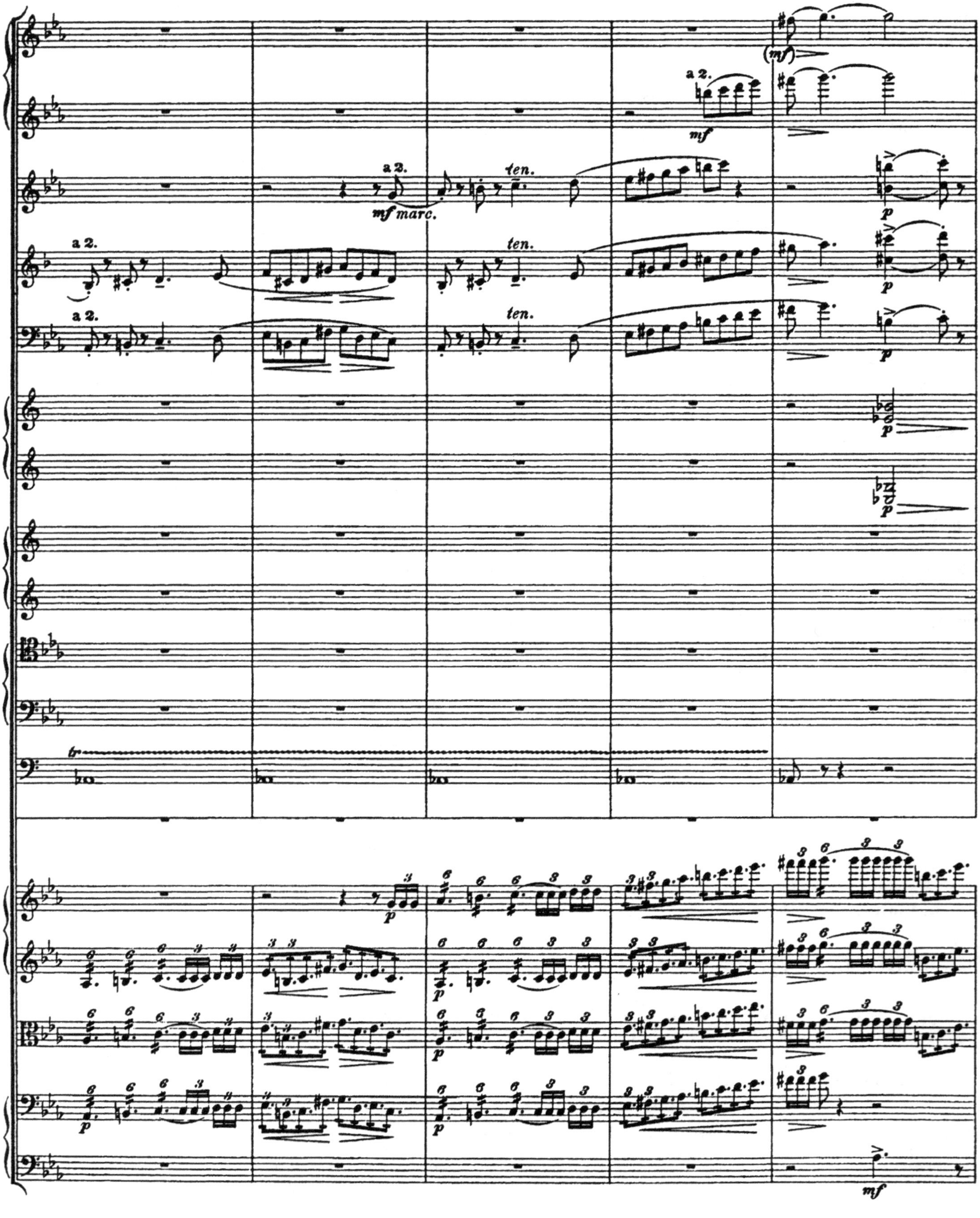
a 2.
mf
a 2.
mf marc.
ten.
a 2.
ten.
a 2.
ten.
p
mf

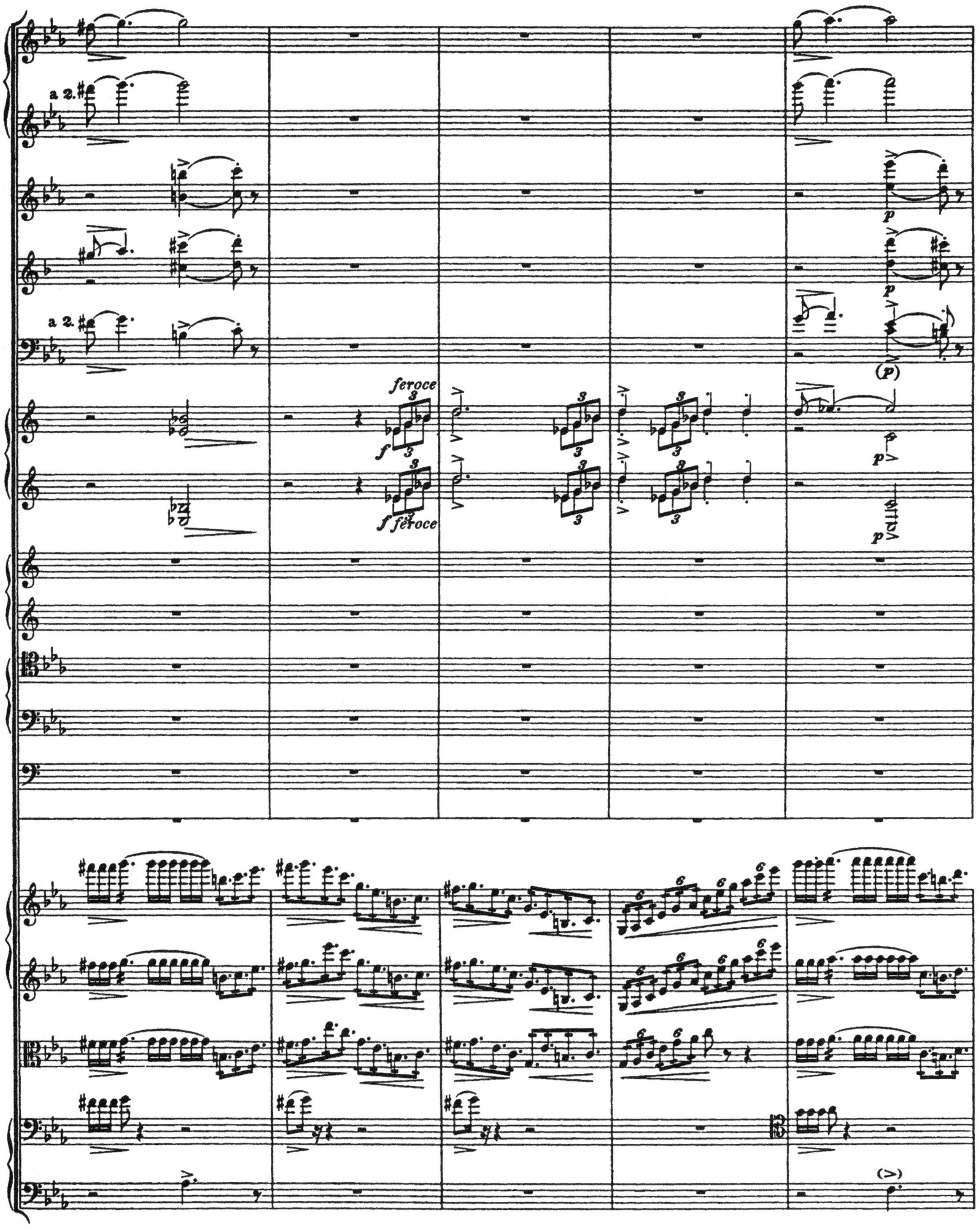
a 2.
a 2.
feroce
f
f feroce
(p)
p
p
(>)

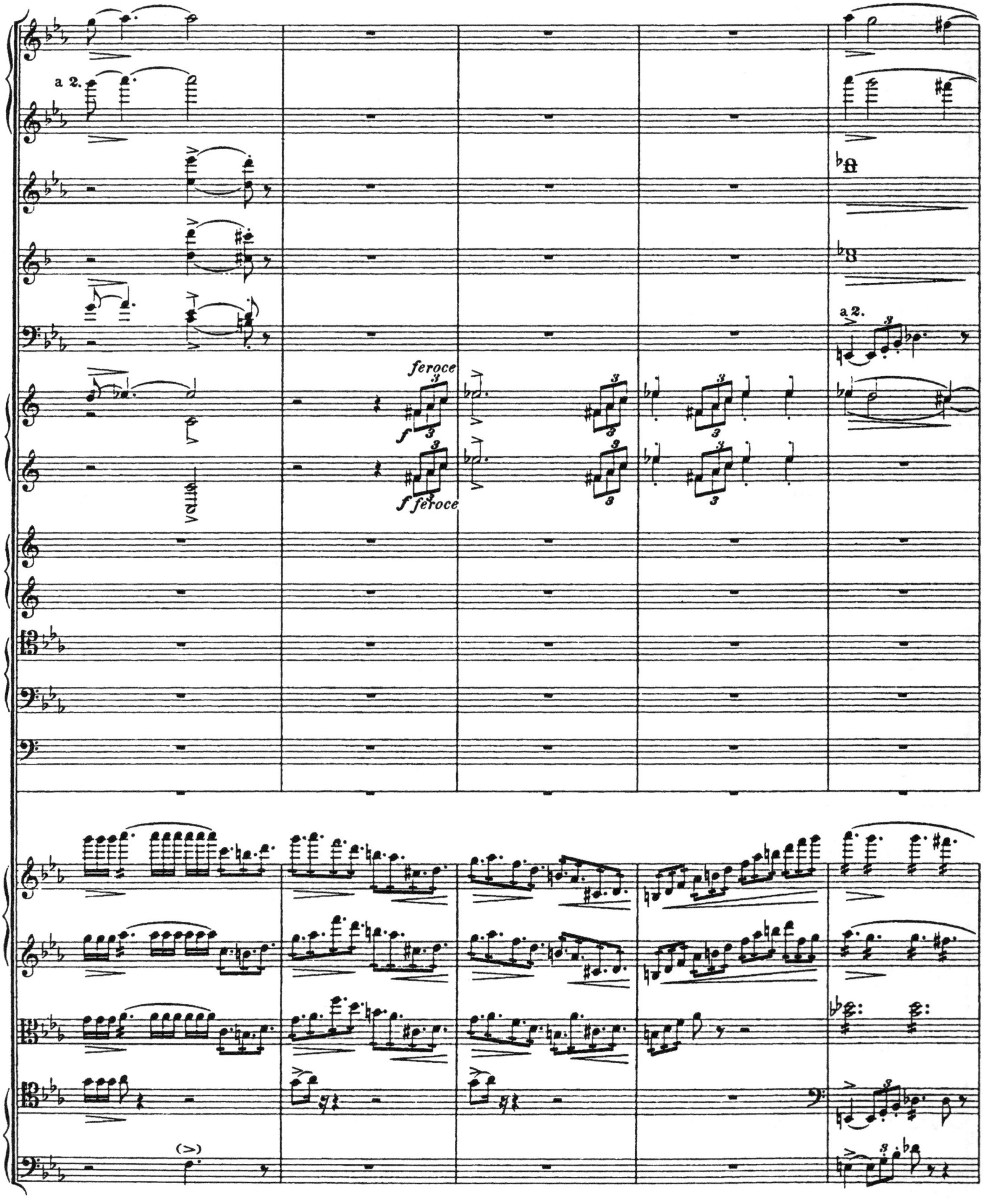
a 2.
a 2.
feroce
f
f feroce
(>)

accelerando
a 2.
cresc.
p
tr
a 2.
3
(mit Holzschlägeln)
(with wooden drum-sticks)
(avec baguettes de bois)
accelerando

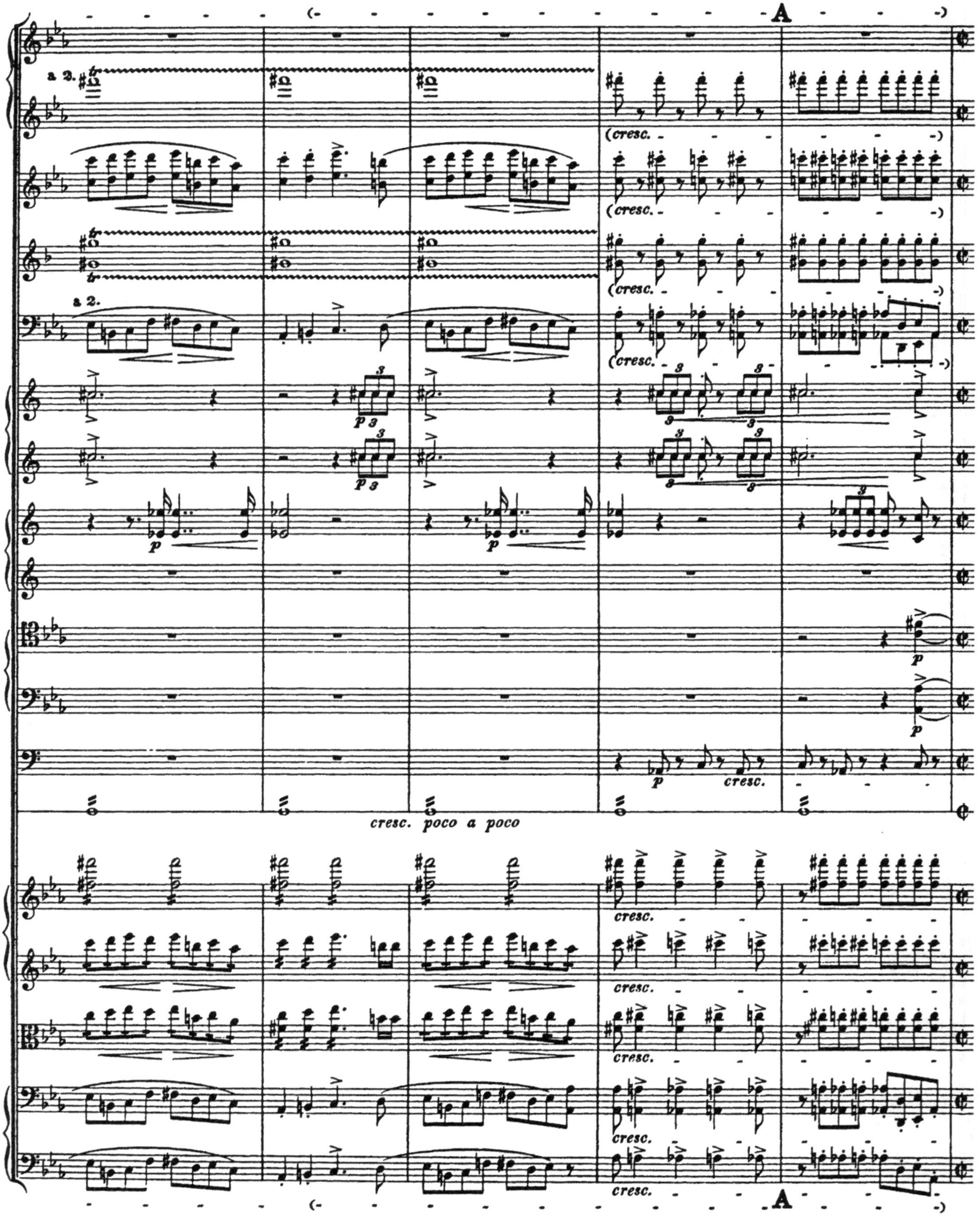
A
a 2.
(cresc.
a 2.
p
cresc.
cresc. poco a poco
A

Von hier an Alla breve taktieren!
From here onwards the beat is Alla breve!
A partir d'ici garder la mesure Alla breve!

Più mosso. (Allegro energico assai.)

Più mosso. (Allegro energico assai.)

NB. Die Triolenfigur sehr schwungvoll mit Bravour gespielt, und die mit > bezeichneten Achtel sehr scharf.
The triplet-figures must be played with great verve and bravura and the quavers marked > be played very pointed.
Les figures de triolets sont jouées avec verve et bravoure, et les croches marquées du signe > avec beaucoup de netteté.

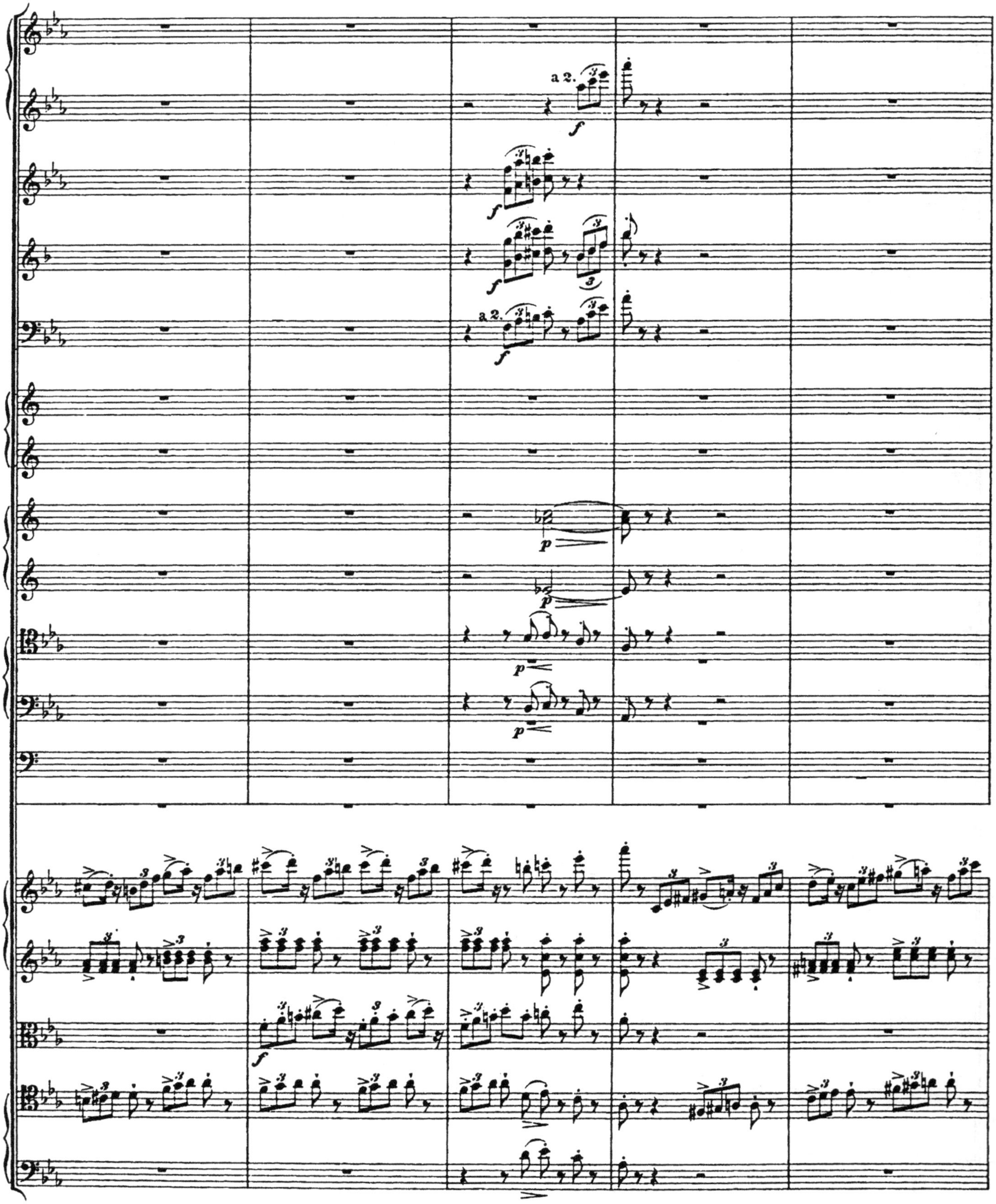
a 2.
a 2.

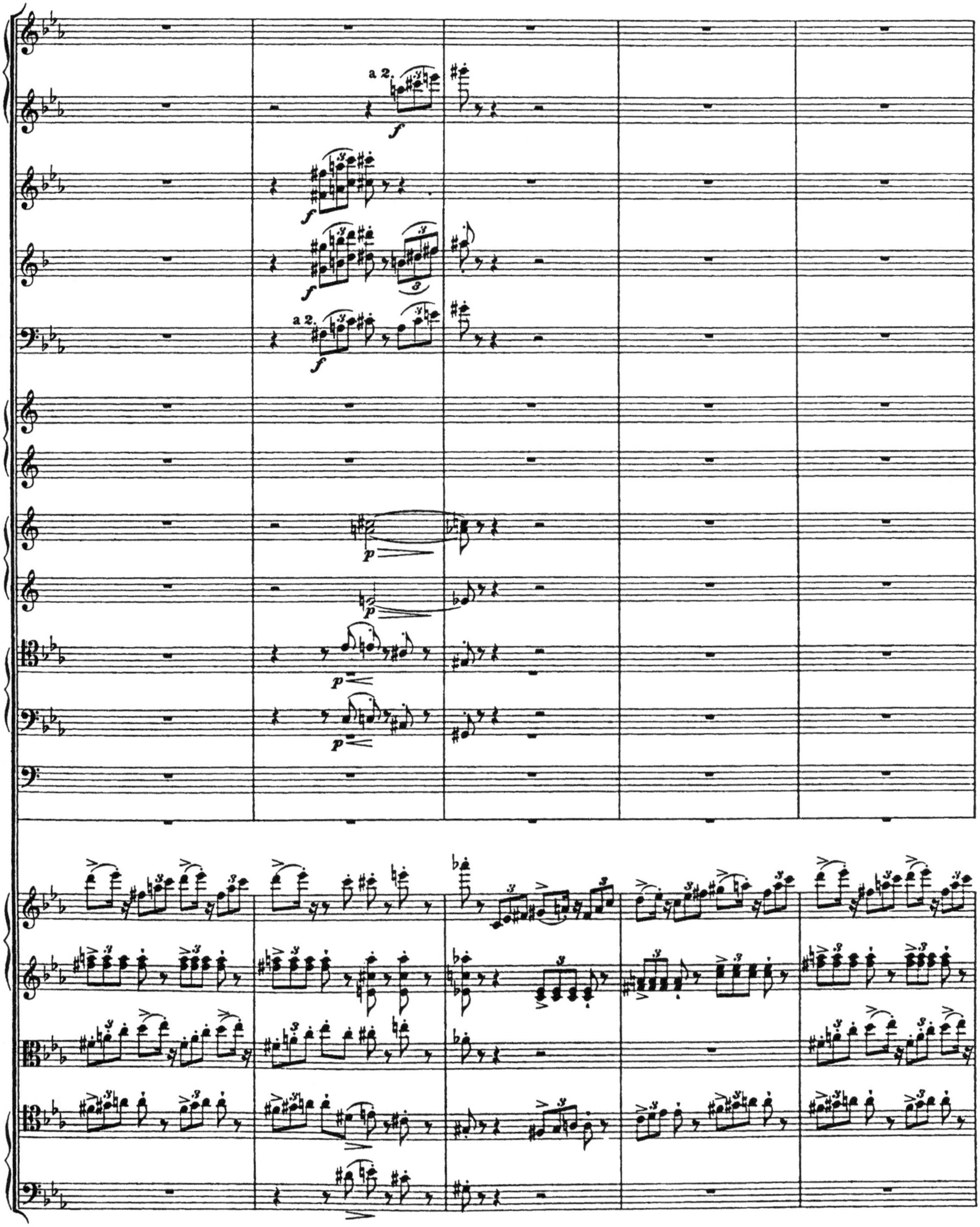
a 2.
f
f
f
a 2.
f
p
p
p
p

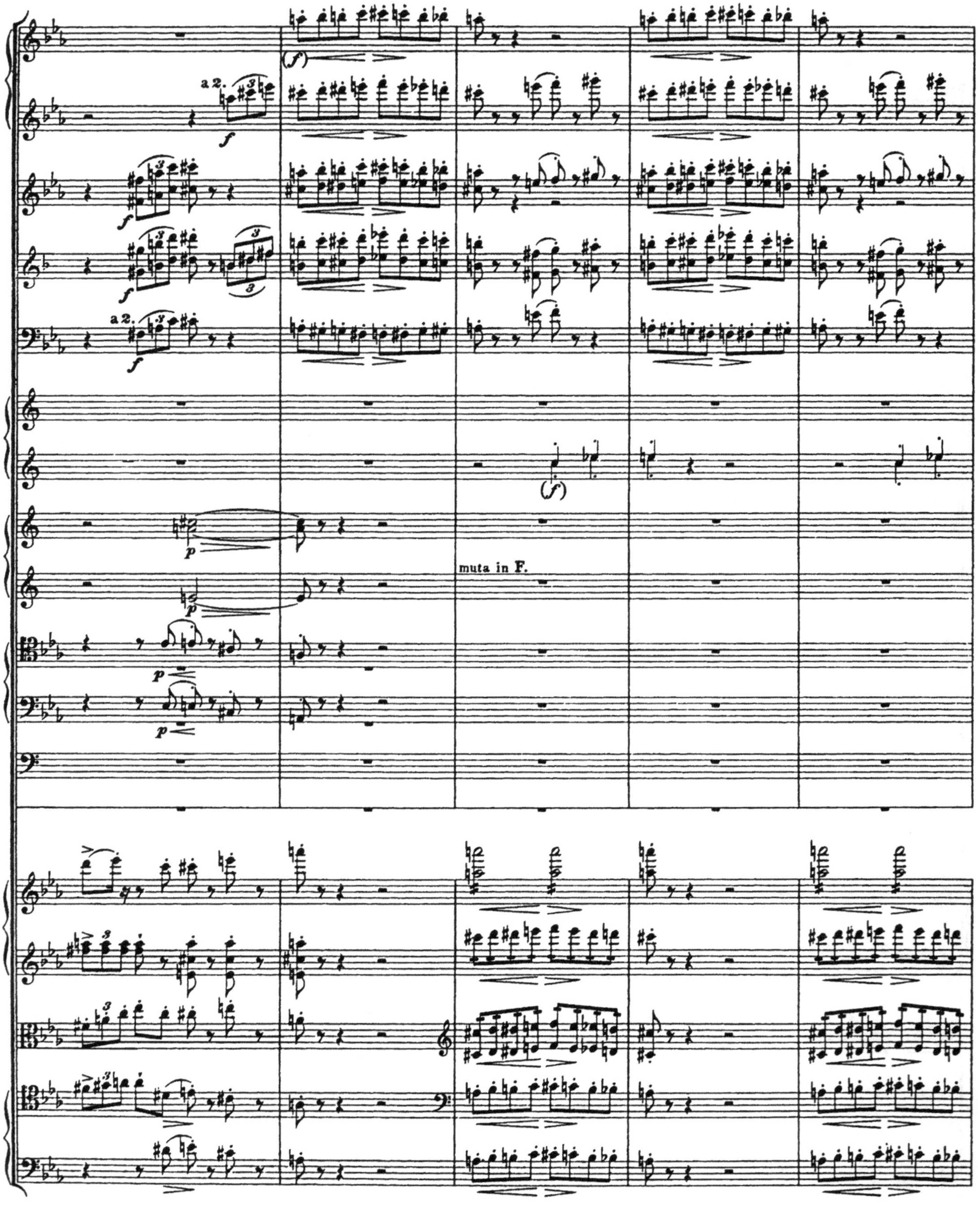
a 2.
a 2.
muta in F.

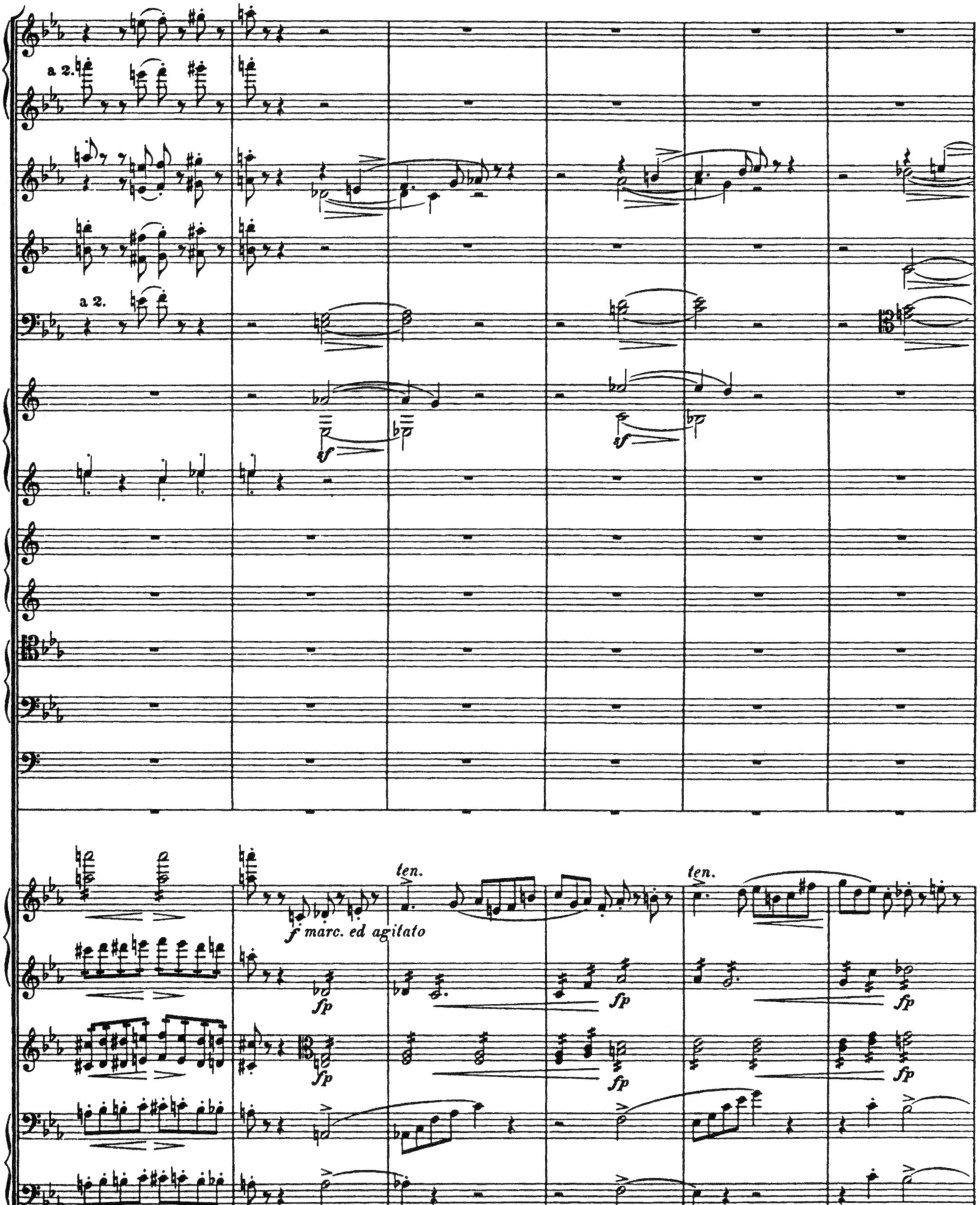
a 2.
a 2.
sf
sf
ten.
ten.
f marc. ed agitato
fp
fp
fp
fp
fp
fp

a 2.
p
cresc.
p
cresc.
p
cresc.
a 2.
p marc.
p
cresc.
p
p
p
p
p
p
p
tr
pp
ten.
ten.
cresc.
fp
cresc.
fp
cresc.
cresc.
cresc.

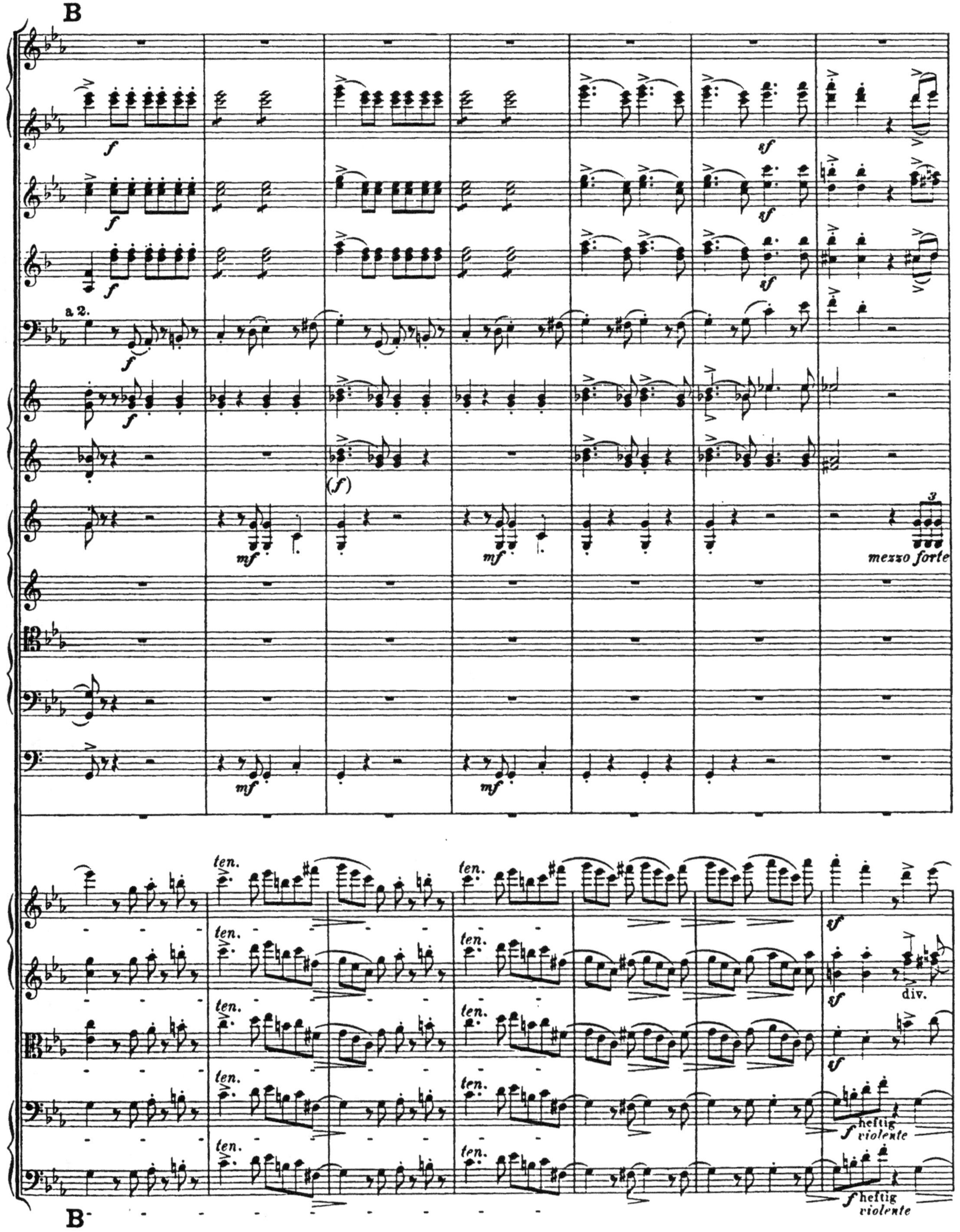
B
f
sf
a 2.
(f)
mf
mezzo forte
ten.
div.
heftig
violente
B

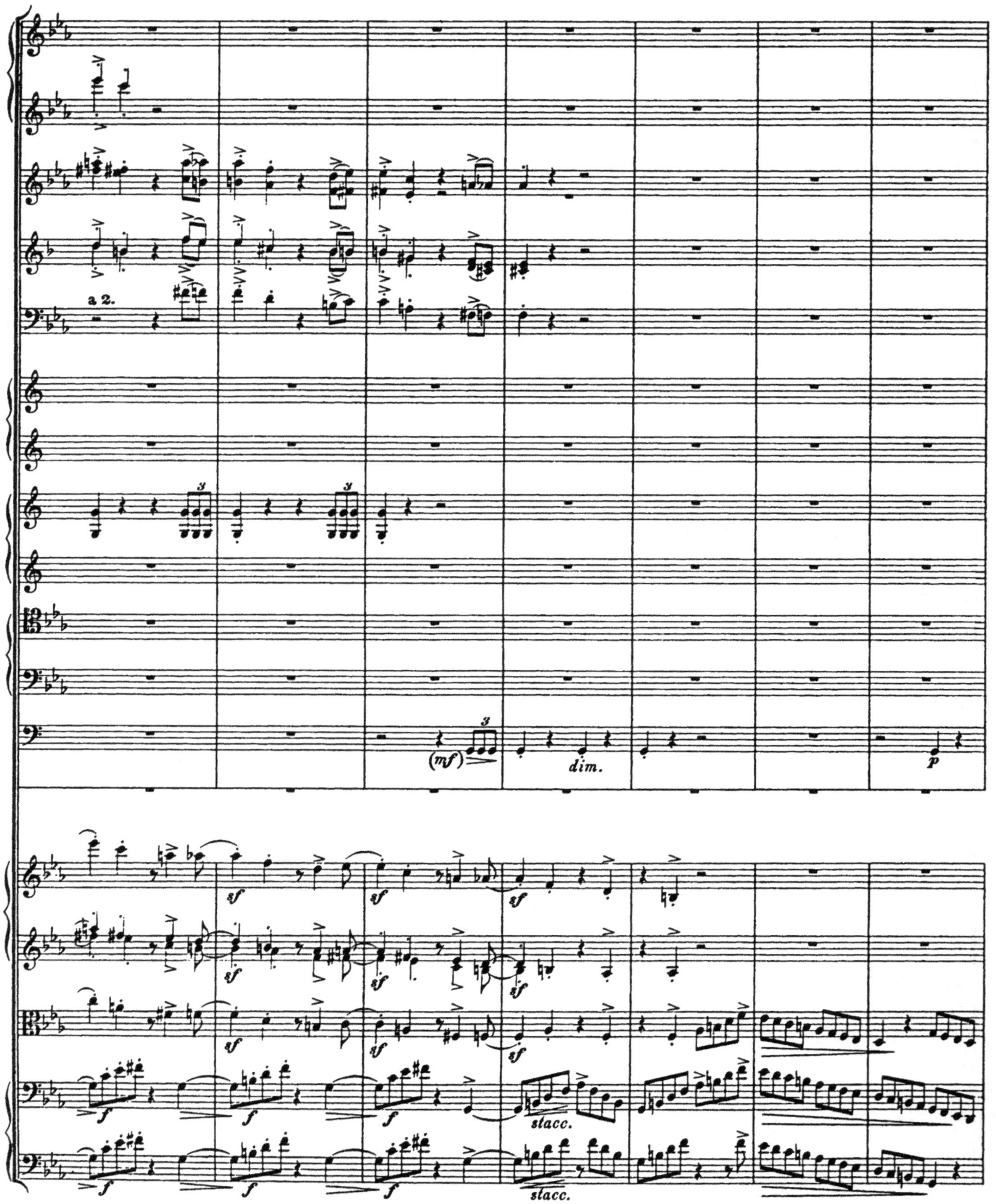
a 2.
(mf)
dim.
p
sf
f
stacc.

a 2. ten.
p marc.
ten.
ten.
sempre piano
tr
pp
sempre pianissimo
p
sempre piano
ten.
p marc.
ten.
ten.
sempre piano
p
pizz.
p

18

a 2.
p stacc.
p stacc.
a 2.
p stacc.
a 2.
p stacc.
a 2.
pizz.
mezzo forte
sf
pizz.
mezzo forte
sf
pizz.
mezzo forte
pizz.
unis.
mezzo forte

4 Viertel! (♩)
Mark the 4 crochets.
Marquez les **4** temps.

Alla breve taktieren! (♩)
Beat alla breve. (♩)
Battez à **2** temps. (♩)

4 Viertel! (♩)
Mark the 4 crochets.
Marquez les **4** temps.

Alla breve taktieren! (♩)
Beat alla breve. (♩)
Battez à **2** temps. (♩)

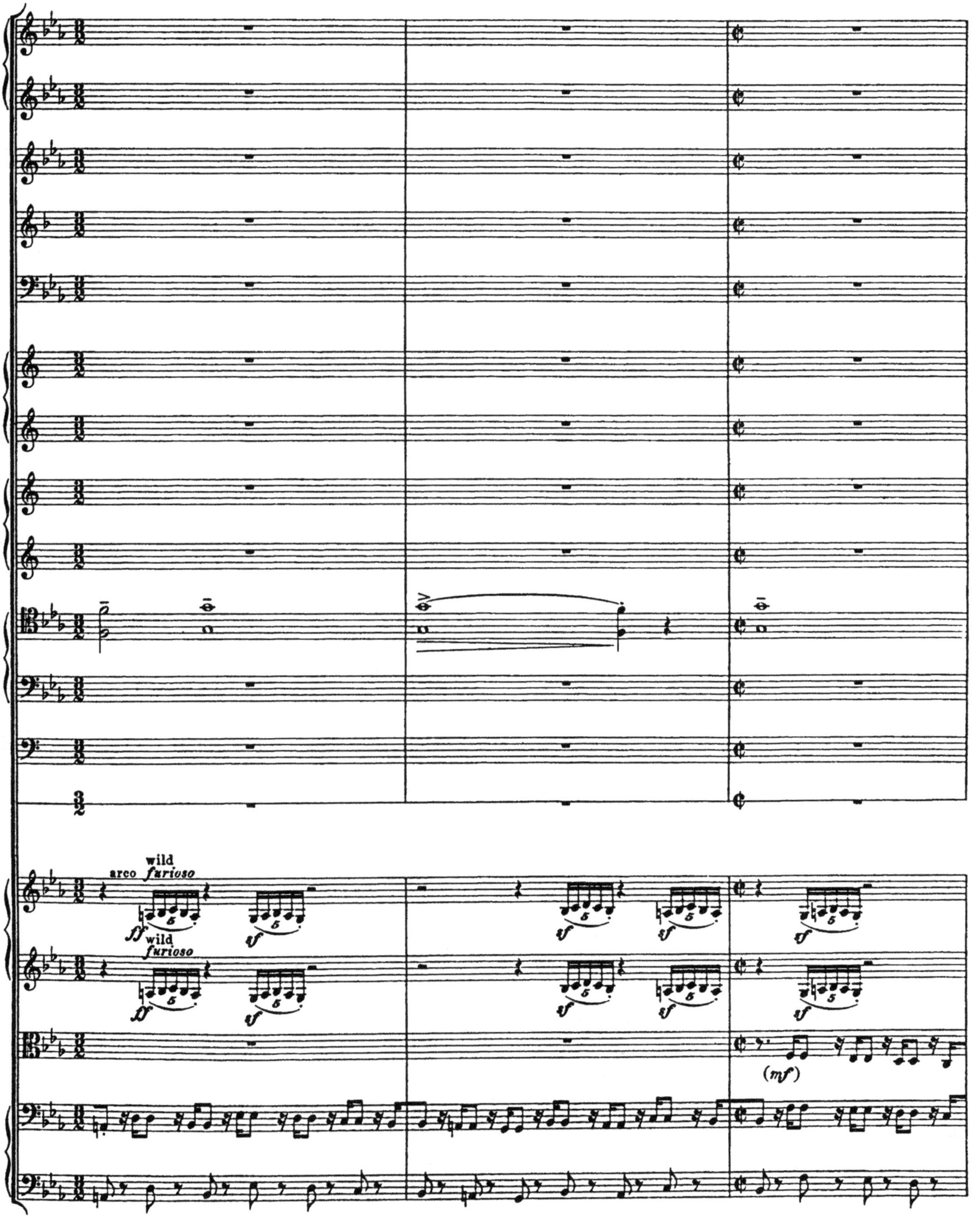

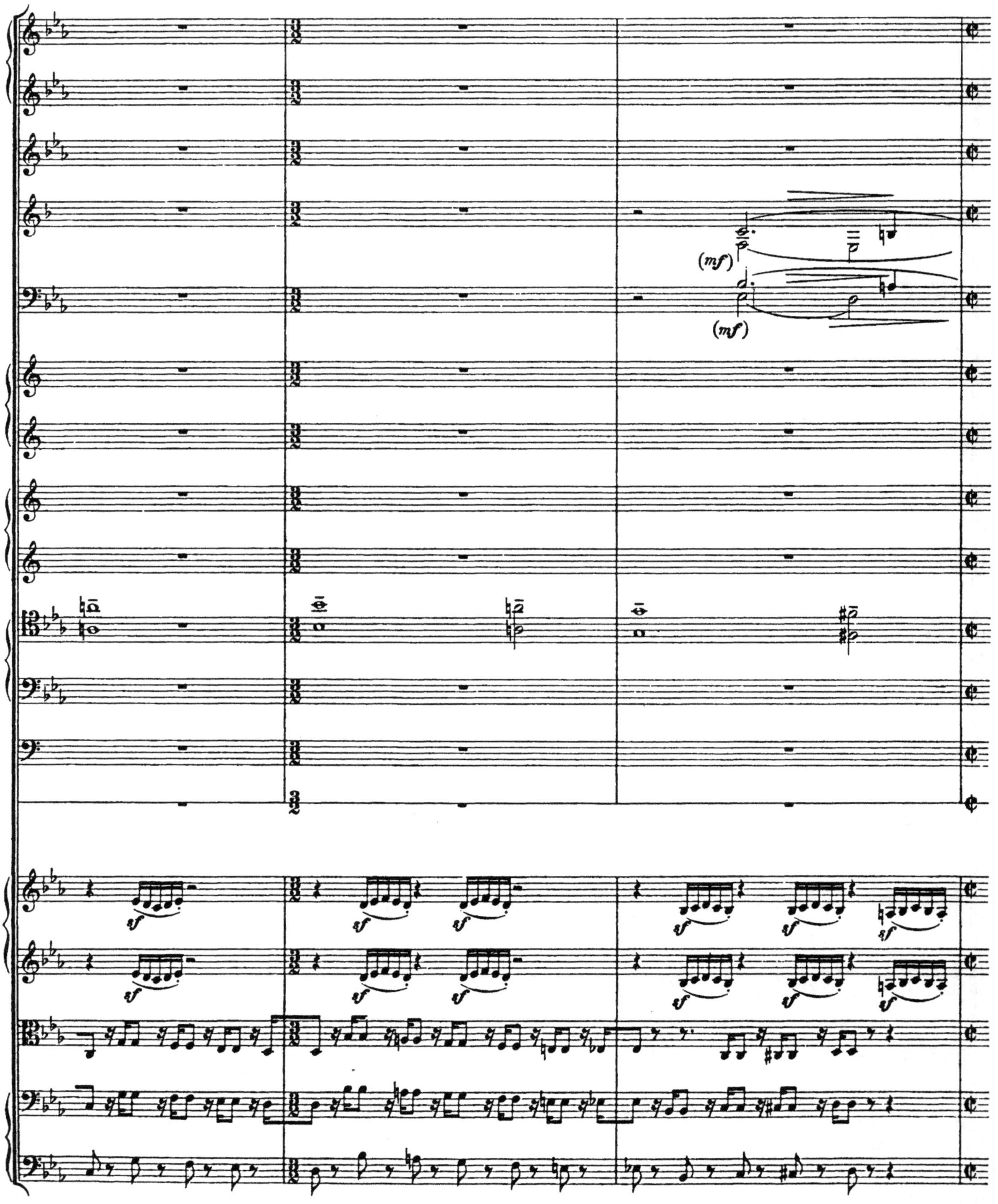
(mf)
(mf)
sf

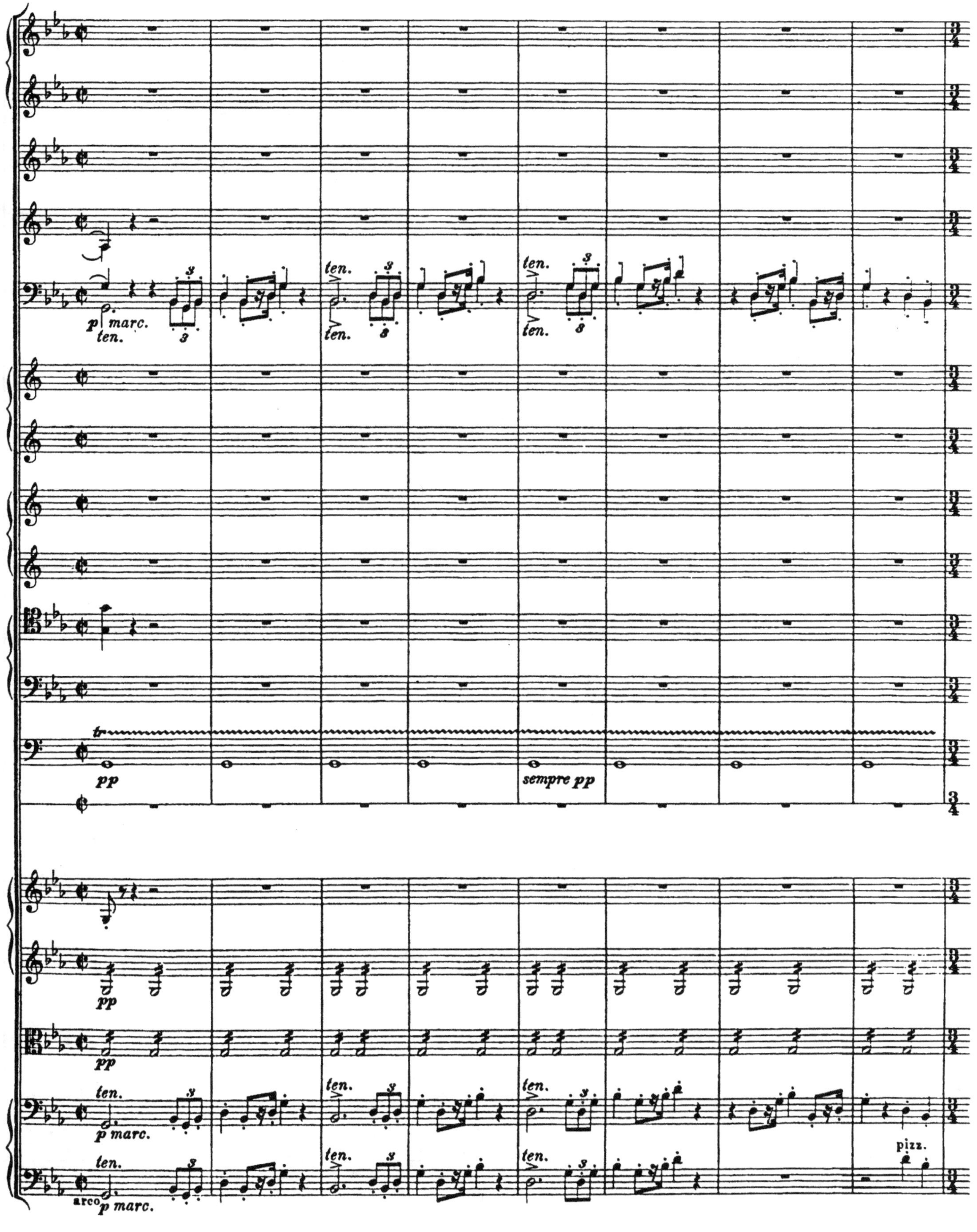
p marc.
ten.
tr
pp
sempre pp
arco
pizz.

24

3 Viertel taktieren! (♩)
Mark the 3 crochets.
Marquez les 3 temps.

3 Viertel taktieren! (♩)
Mark the 3 crochets.
Marquez les 3 temps.

40314

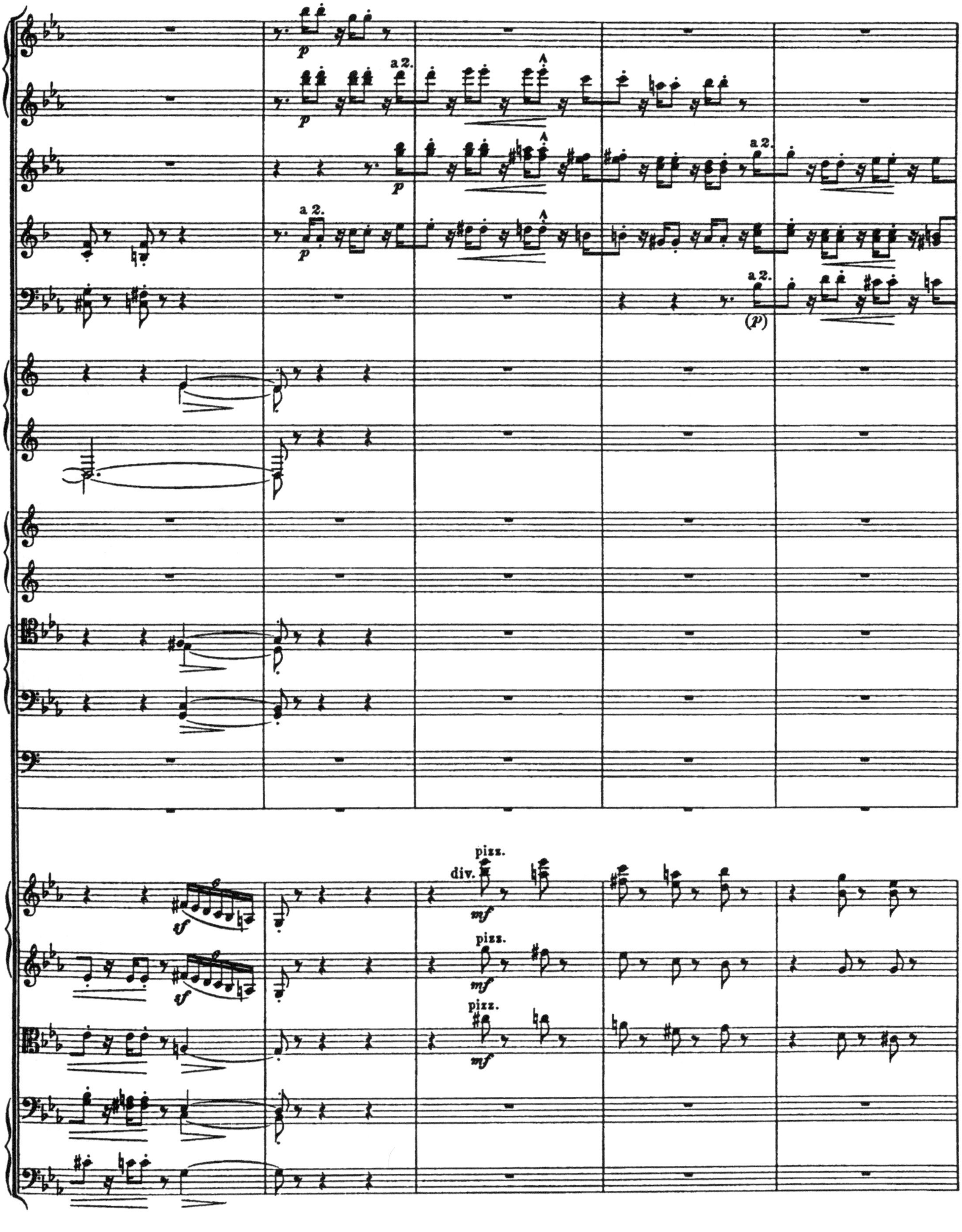
p
a 2.
p
p
a 2.
p
a 2.
(p)
pizz.
div.
mf
sf
pizz.
mf
sf
pizz.
mf

4 Viertel! (♩)
Mark the 4 crochets.
Marquez les 4 temps.

Alla breve! (♩)
Beat alla breve. (♩)
Battez à 2 temps. (♩)

4 Viertel! (♩)
Mark the 4 crochets.
Marquez les 4 temps.

Alla breve! (♩)
Beat alla breve. (♩)
Battez à 2 temps. (♩)

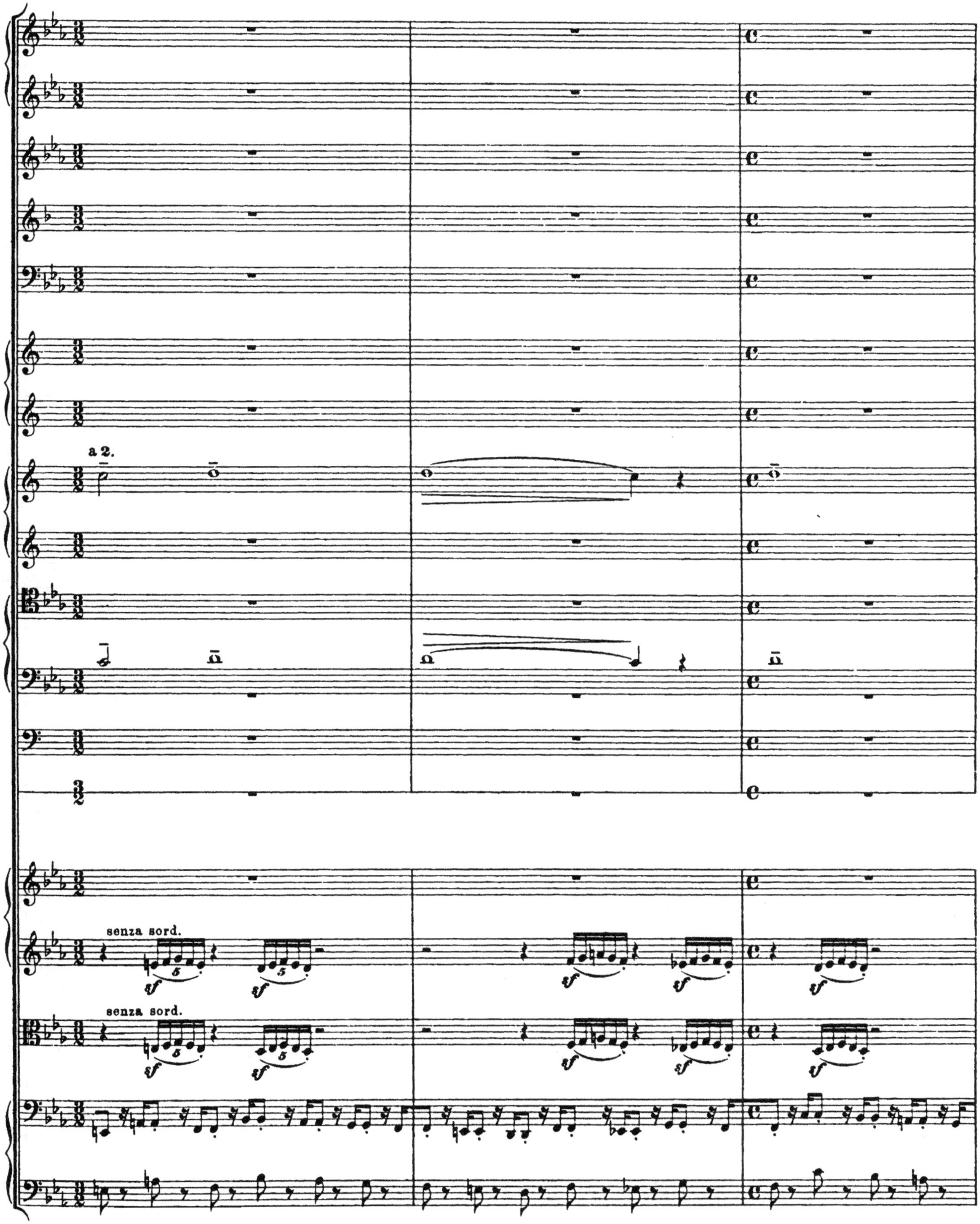
a 2.
senza sord.
sf
senza sord.
sf

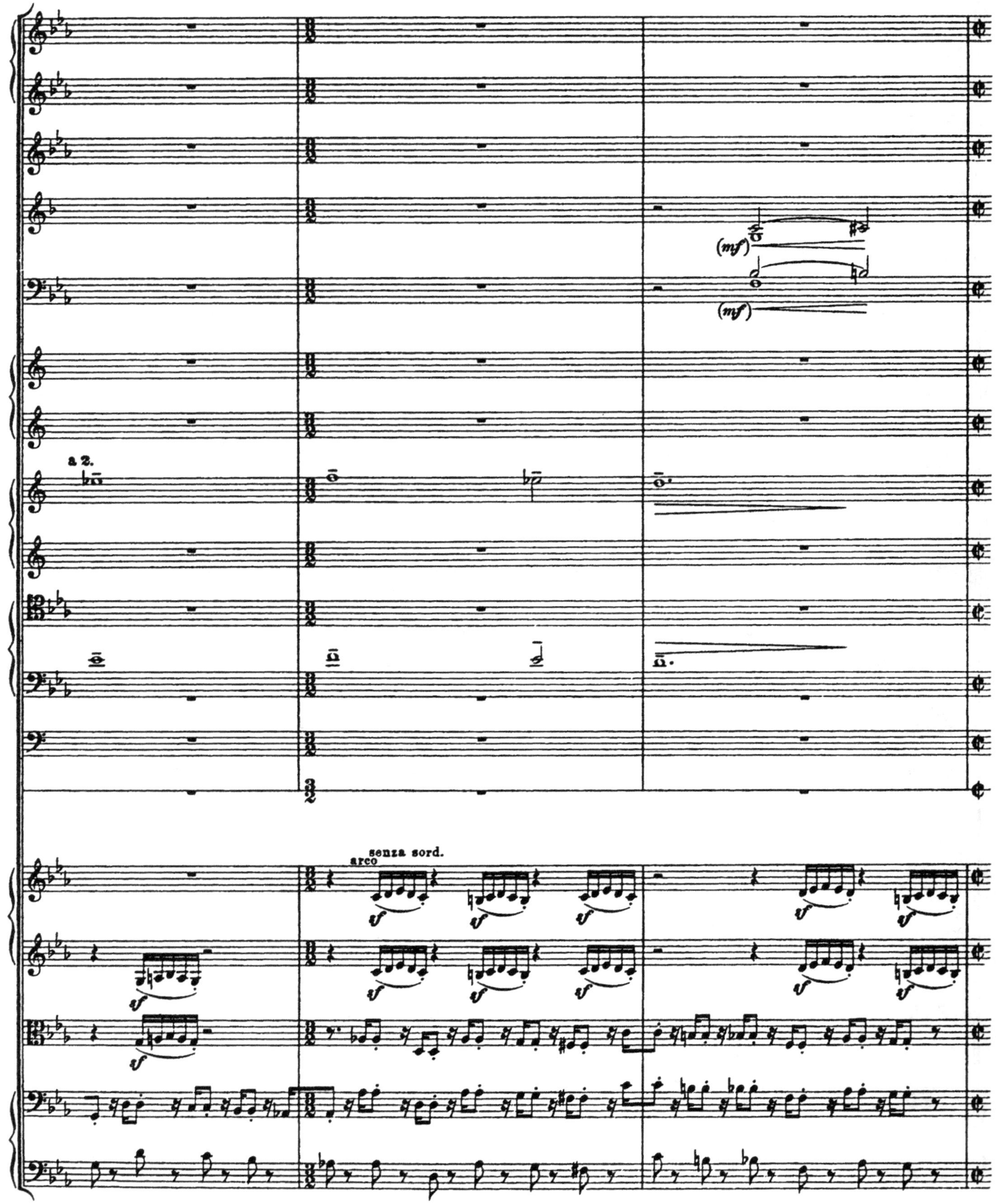
(mf)
(mf)
a 2.
senza sord.
arco
sf

D Immer alla breve taktieren!
Continue beating alla breve.
Battez toujours à 2 temps.

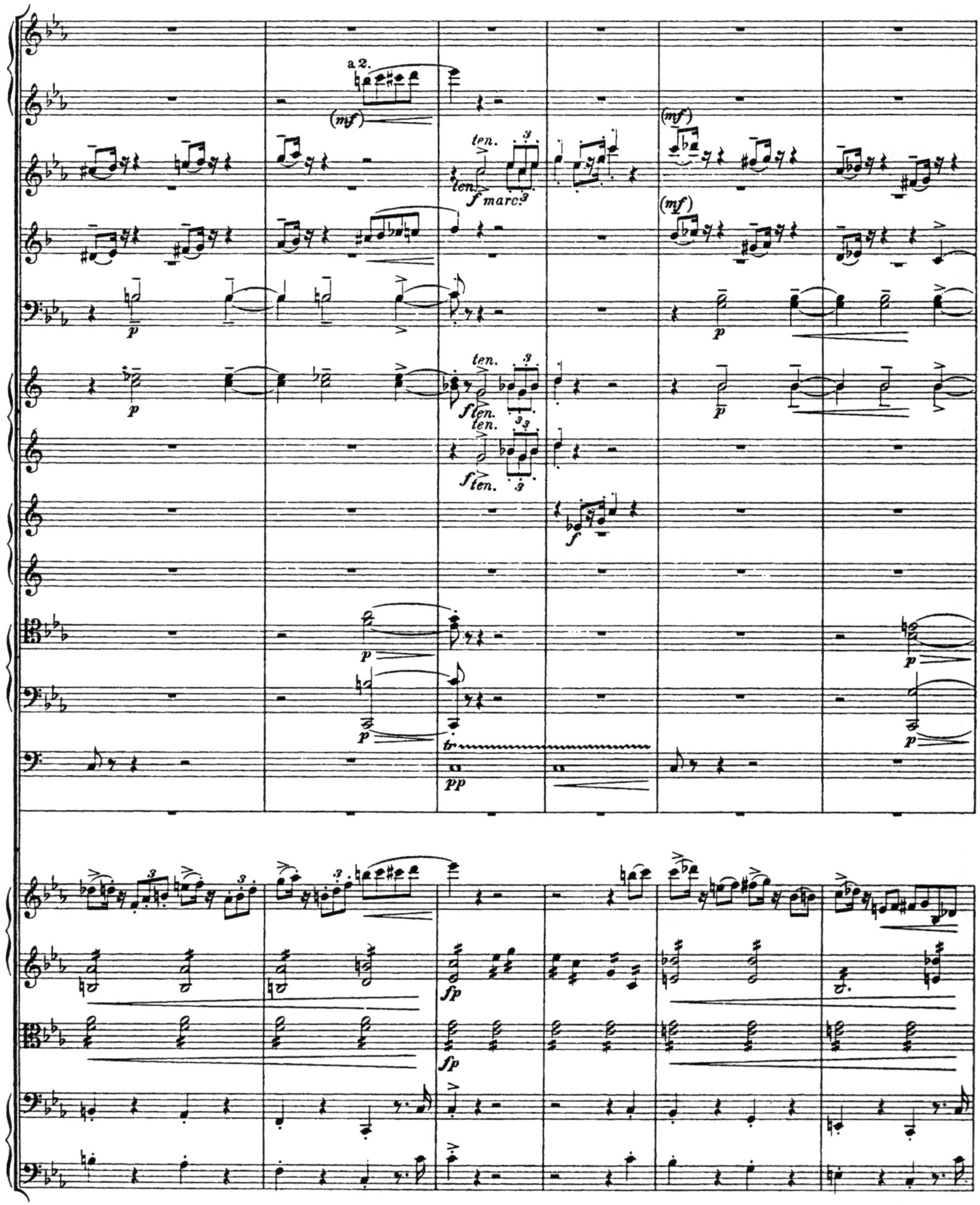
a 2.
(mf)
ten.
f marc.
(mf)
(mf)
p
p
p
ten.
f ten.
ten.
f ten.
f
p
p
p
p
tr
pp
fp
fp

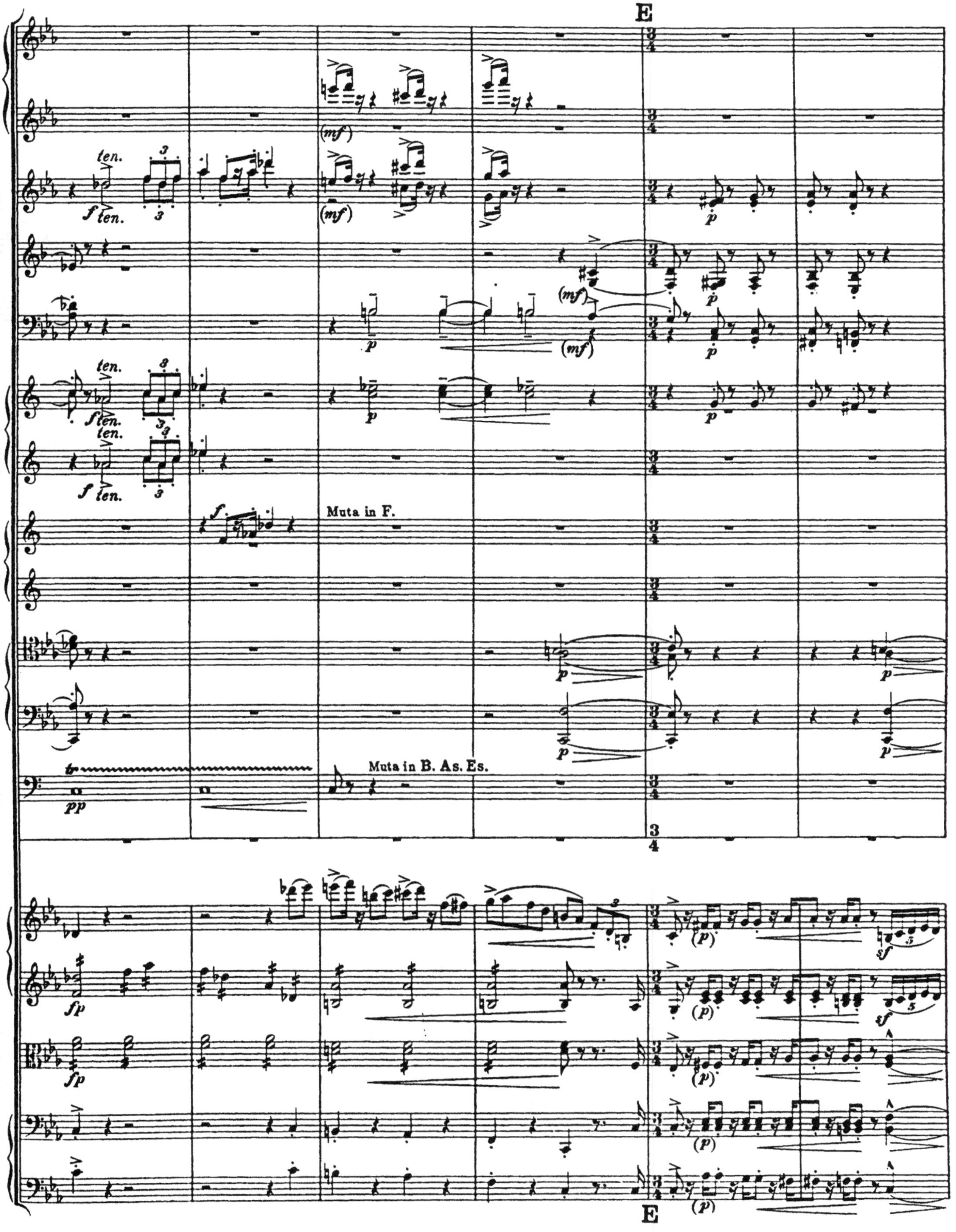
E
ten.
f ten.
(mf)
(mf)
p
(mf)
Muta in F.
Muta in B. As. Es.
pp
fp
(p)
sf
E

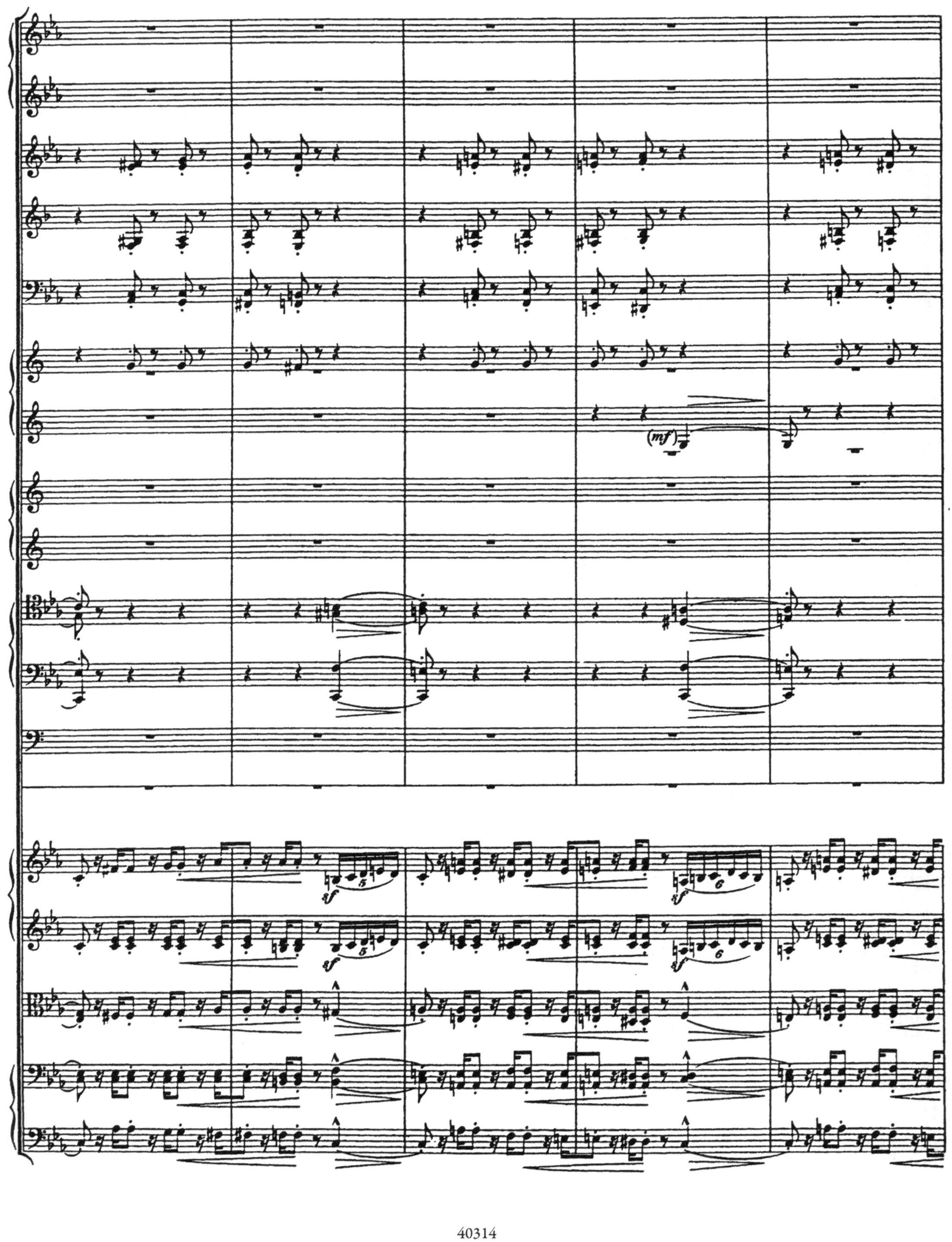
(mf)
sf
5
6

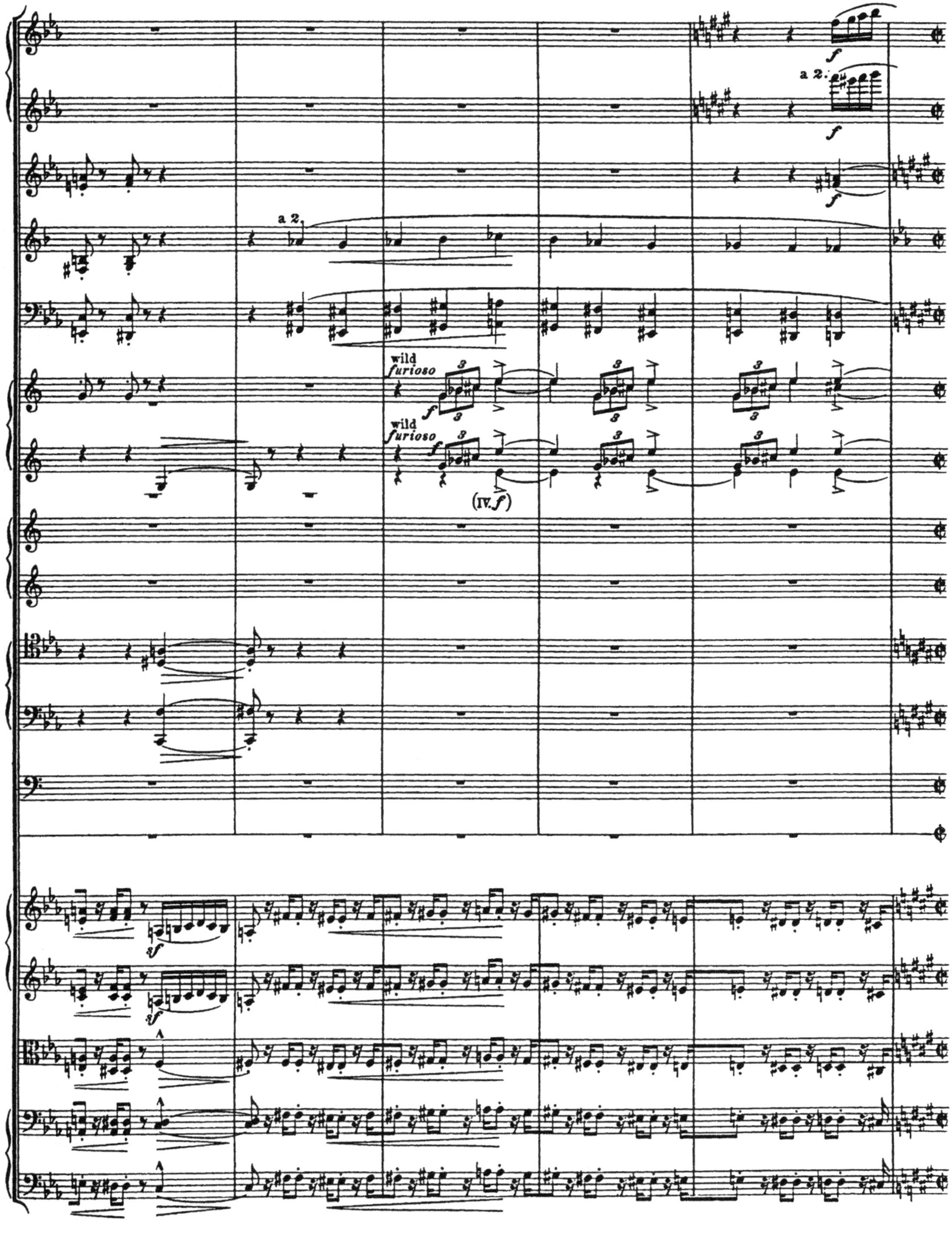
a 2.
a 2.
wild
furioso
wild
furioso
(IV. f)

Alla breve.
Poco a poco accelerando (sin al Andante maestoso).

Poco a poco accelerando (sin al Andante maestoso).
Alla breve.

mit Paukenschlägeln
with drumsticks
avec baguettes de timbale

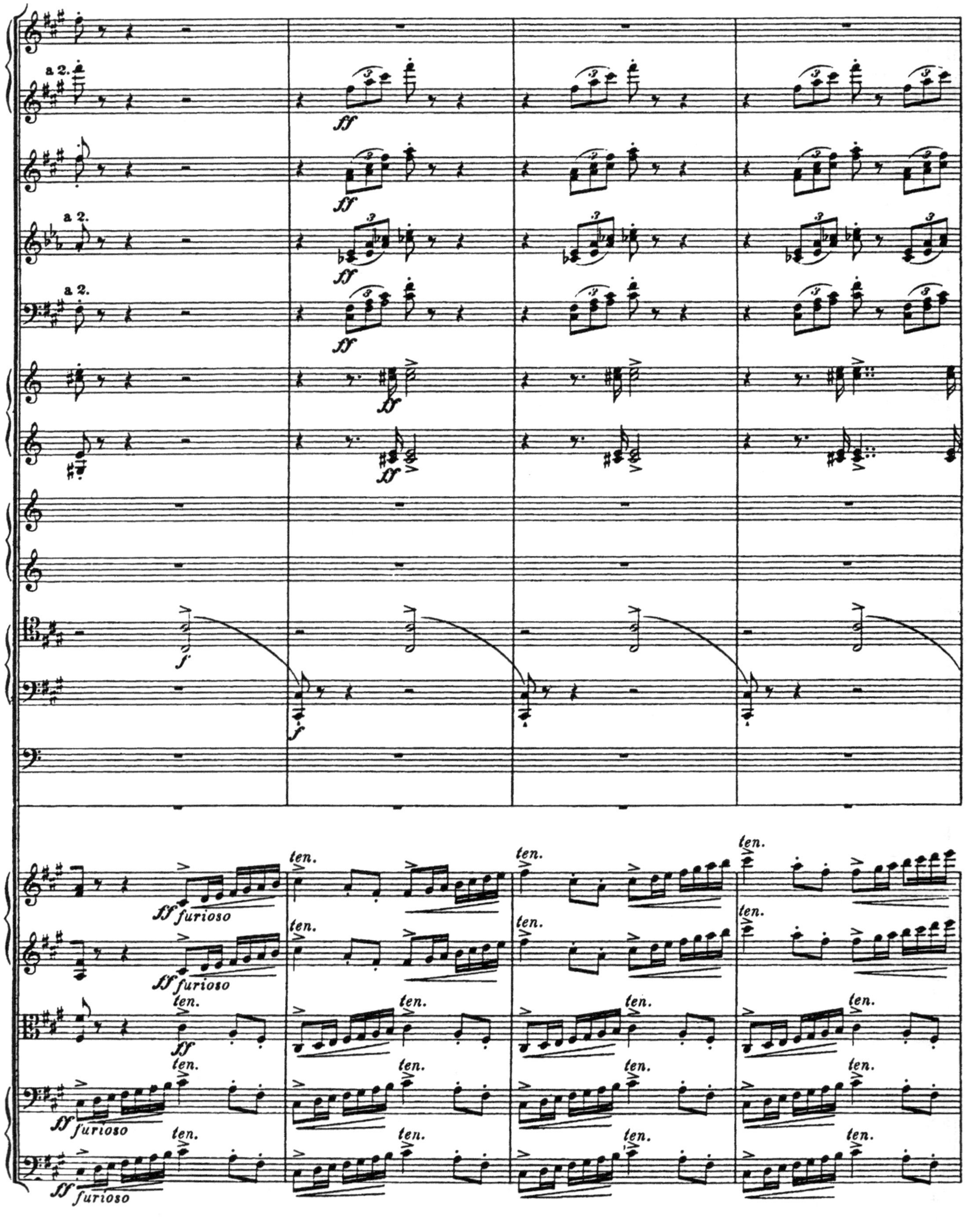
a 2.
ff
a 2.
a 2.
f
ff furioso
ten.
ff

a 2.
ff
ff
ff
ff
a 2.
ff
ff
ff
in F.
ten.
(Schlachtruf.)
(War-cry.)
(Cri de guerre.)
ff
ff
ff
ten.
(Schlachtruf.)
(War-cry.)
(Cri de guerre.)
ff
(II. ff)
(Tb. ff)
rinf.
rinf.

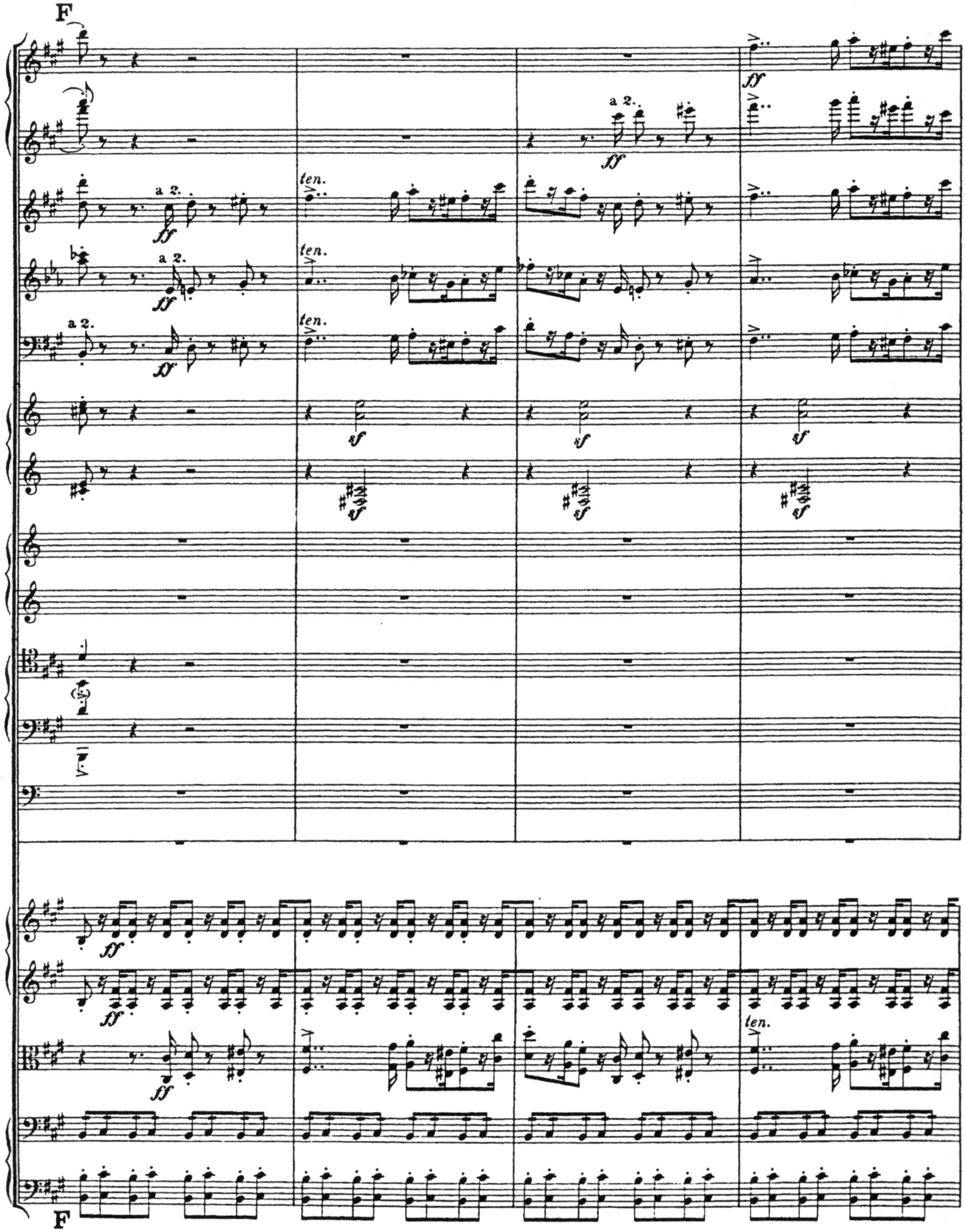
F
a 2.
ff
ten.
sf
F

a 2.
a 2.
a 2.
a 2.
mit Paukenschlägeln
with drumsticks
(f)
avec baguettes de timbale

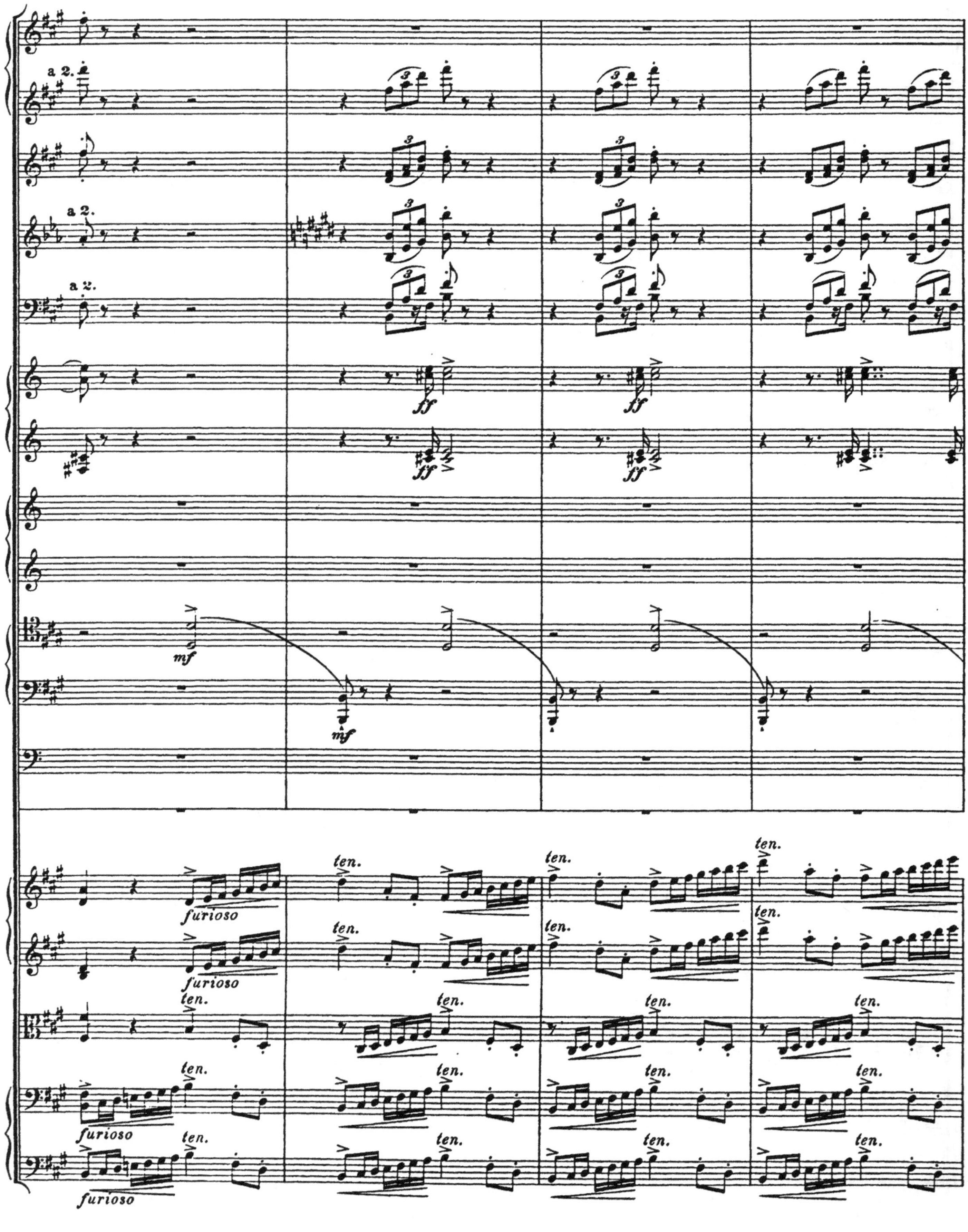
a 2.
a 2.
a 2.
ff
ff
ff
ff
mf
mf
furioso
furioso
furioso
furioso
ten.

a 2.
a 2.
a 2.
a 2.
ten.
ff
(Schlachtruf.)
(War-cry.)
ten. (Cri de guerre.)
ten.
ff
ten.
(Schlachtruf.)
(War-cry.)
(Cri de guerre.)
ten.
f
(f)
tr
tr
rinf.
rinf.

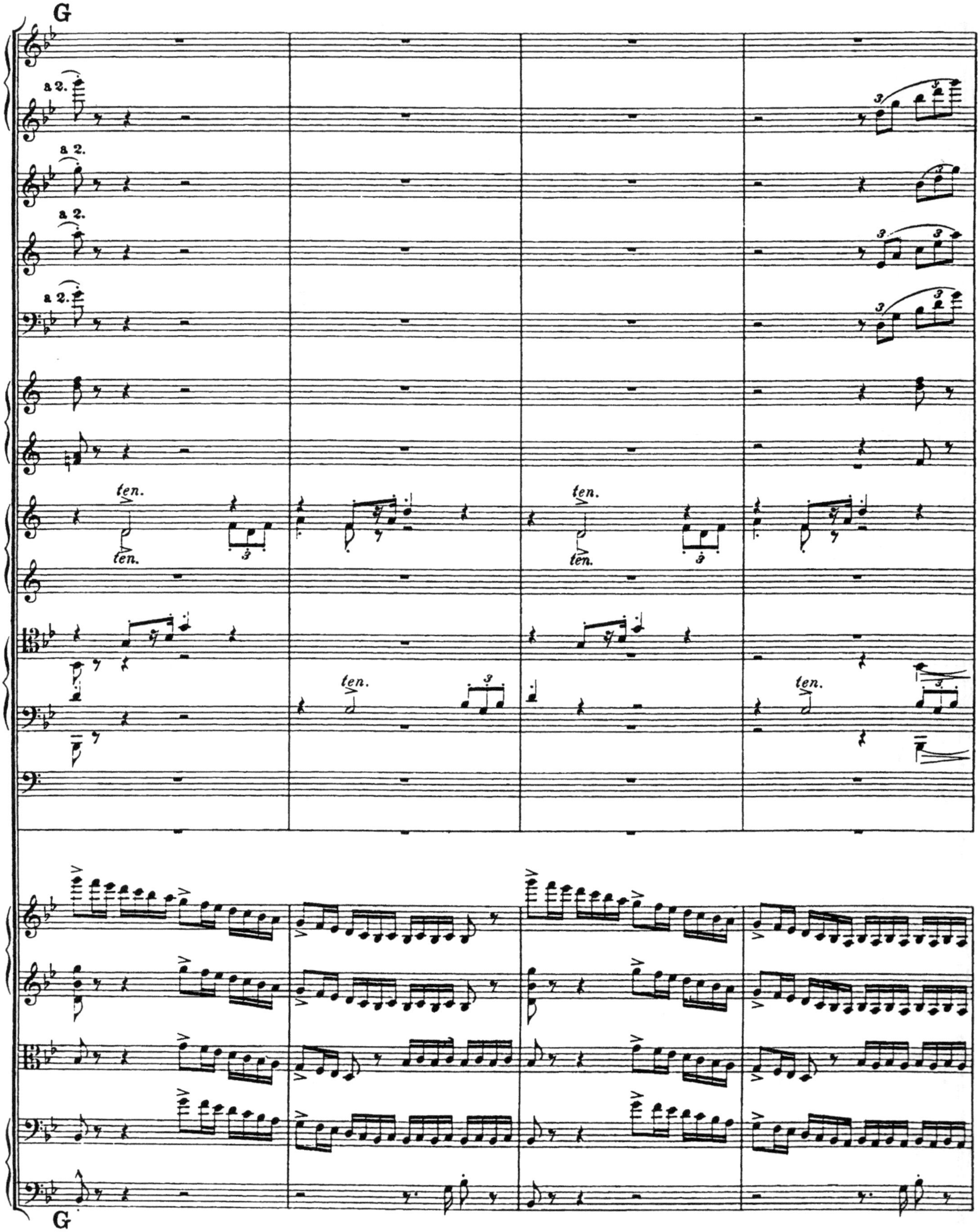
G
a 2.
a 2.
a 2.
a 2.
ten.
ten.
ten.
ten.
ten.
ten.
3
3
3
3
G

Immer stürmischer bis zum Buchstaben **H**.
More and more stormily up to the letter H.
De plus en plus impétueux jusqu'à la lettre **H**.

Immer stürmischer bis zum Buchstaben **H**.
More and more stormily up to the letter H.
De plus en plus impétueux jusqu'à la lettre **H**.

a 2.
(mf) cresc.
(mf) cresc.
(mf) cresc.
ff
ff
a 2.
(cresc.)
cresc.
cresc.
Solo
mf
(mf)
tr
cresc.
trem.
p
cresc.
cresc.
ff
cresc.
ff
cresc.
ff
cresc.
ff
cresc.

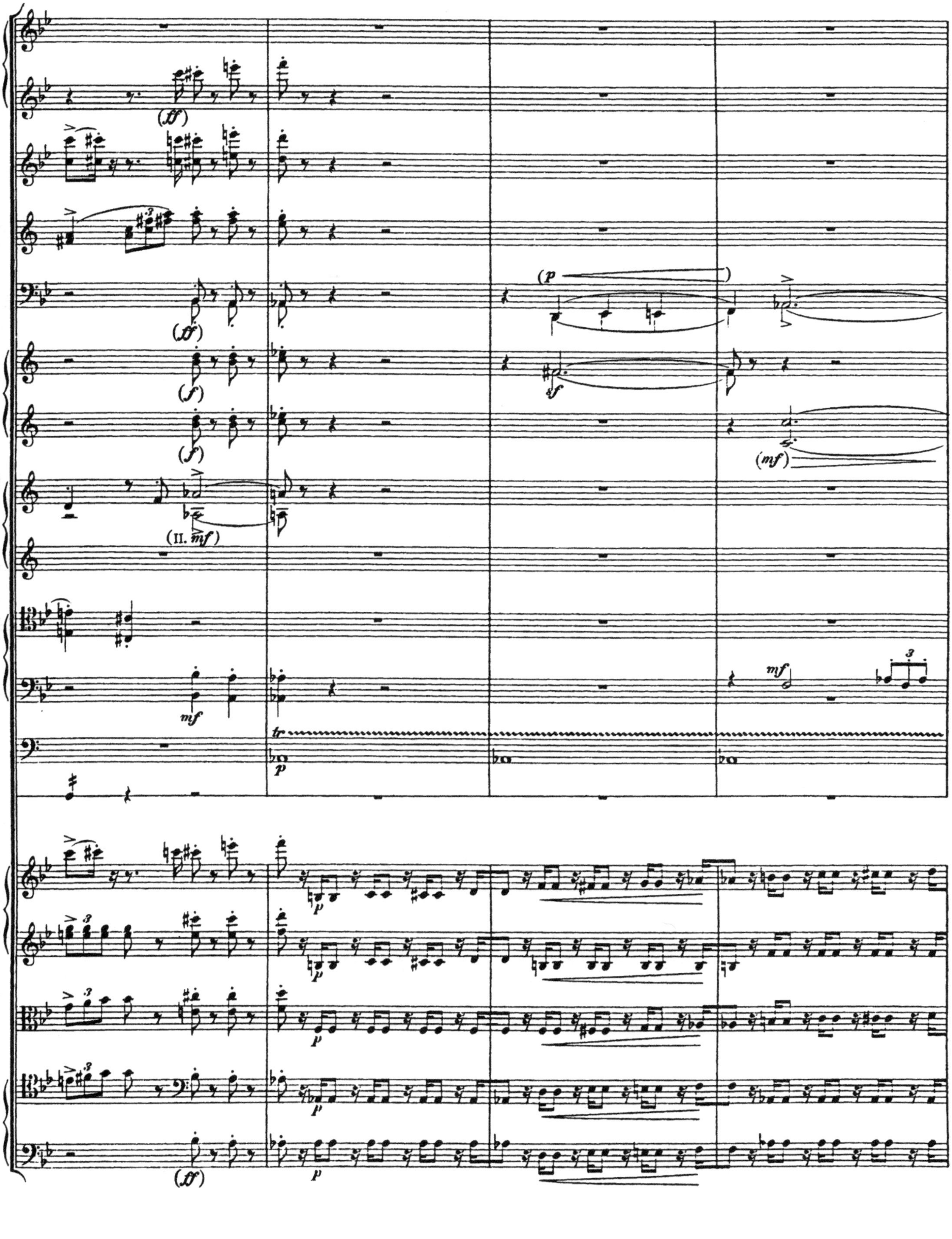
(ff)
(ff)
(p
)
(f)
sf
(f)
(mf)
(II. mf)
mf
mf
tr
p
p
p
p
p
p
(ff)

a 2.
(mf) cresc.
(mf) cresc.
ff
(mf) cresc.
ff
(cresc.
cresc.
Solo
f
(p) cresc.
mf
tr
cresc.
trem.
p
cresc.
cresc.
cresc.
cresc.
cresc.

H
ff sempre
a 2.
(ff)
ff sempre
ff sempre
a 2.
ff sempre
a 2.
ff sempre
a 2.
(ff)
ff (sempre)
(f)
ff (sempre)
(f)
ff (sempre)
(II. f)
ff (sempre)
(mf)
ff sempre
mf
ff sempre
cresc.
ff sempre
ff sempre
ff sempre
ff sempre
(ff)
H
ff sempre

a 2.
a 2.
a 2.
stacc.
a 2.
stacc.
f
(mit breitem Strich)
(whole bows)
(tout l'archet)
fff
marc.
(mit breitem Strich)
(whole bows)
(tout l'archet)
ff
marc.
(mit breitem Strich)
(whole bows)
(tout l'archet)
ff
marc.
ff
ff
ff

a 2.
a 2.
(mit breitem Strich)
(whole bows)
(tout l'archet)
fff
fff
marc.
marc.
ff
ff
ff
f

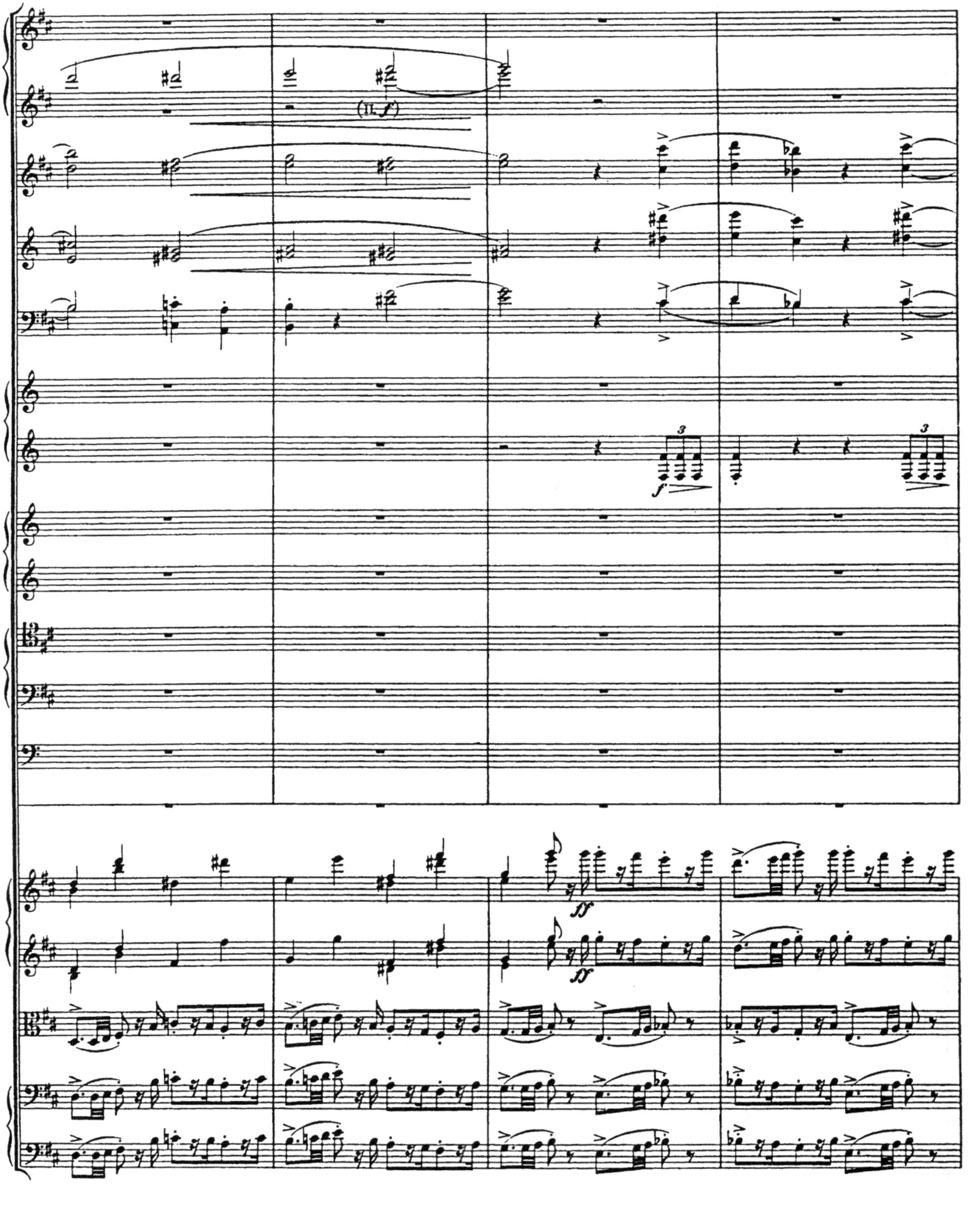
(II. f)
f
ff
ff

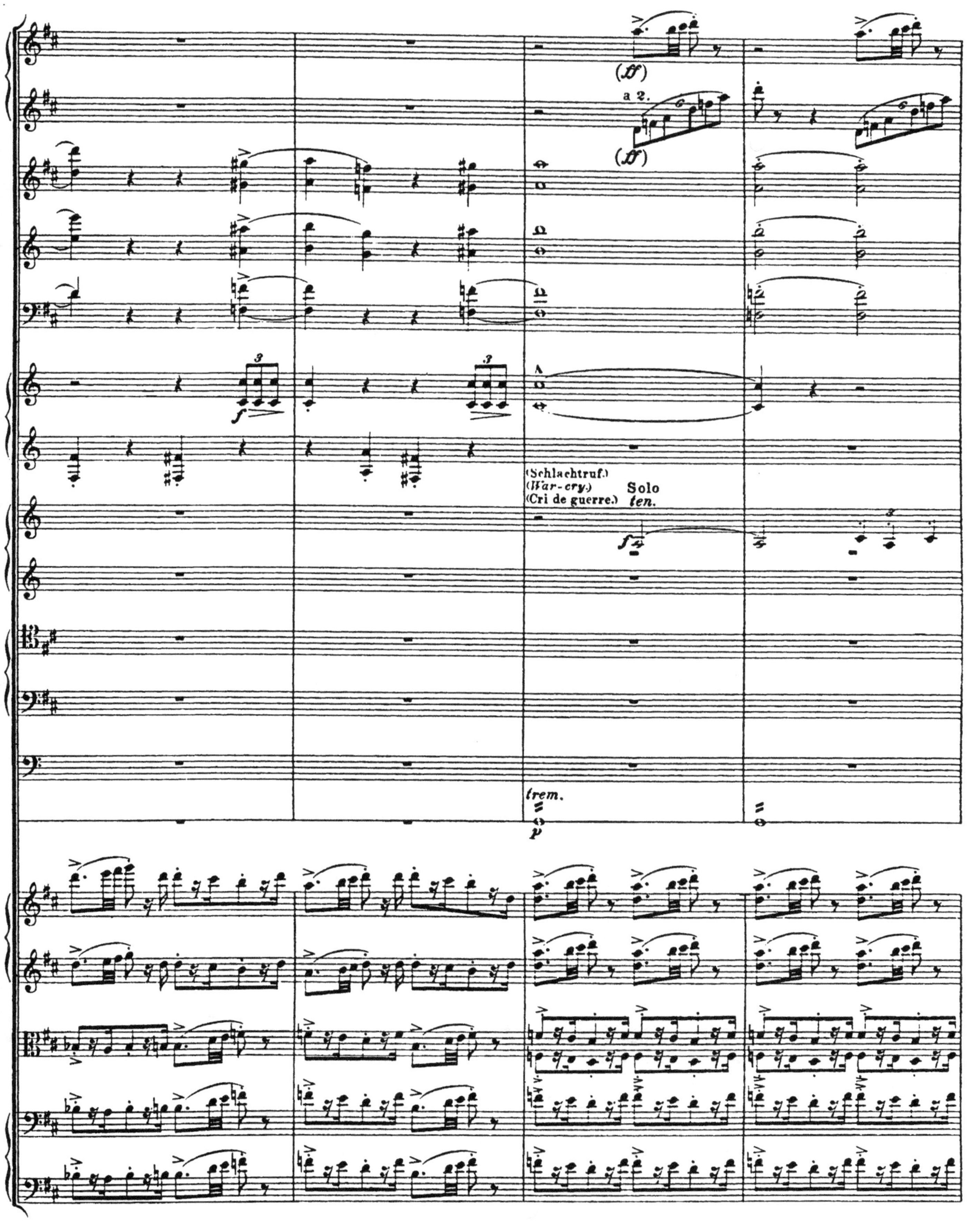
(ff)
a 2.
(ff)
f
(Schlachtruf.)
(War-cry.)
(Cri de guerre.)
Solo
ten.
f
trem.
p

cresc. poco a poco

a 2.
a 2.
a 2.
a 2.
mit Holzschlägeln
with wooden sticks
avec baguettes de bois
unis.

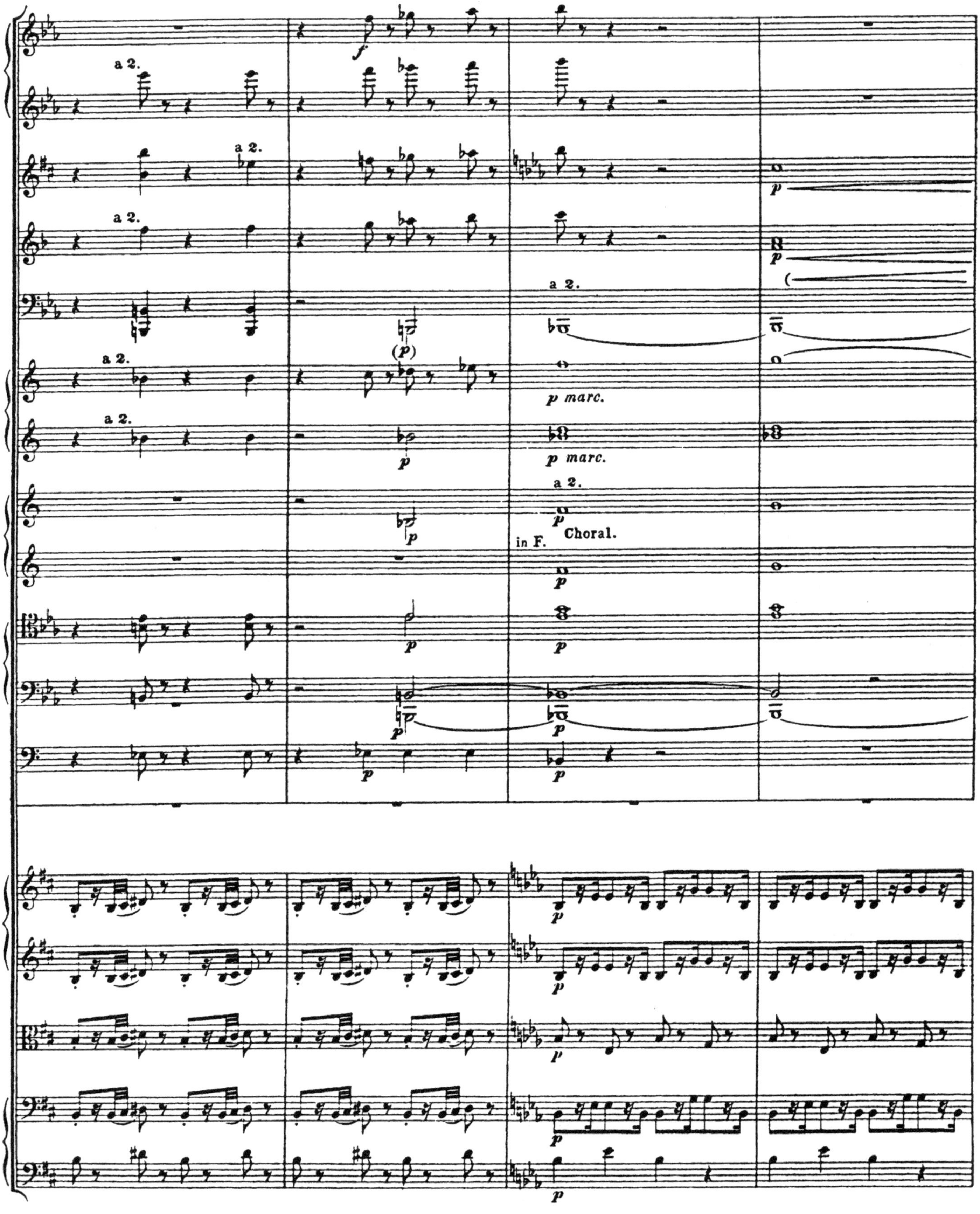
a 2.
a 2.
a 2.
a 2.
a 2.
a 2.
a 2.
p marc.
p marc.
in F.
Choral.

a 2.
a 2.
a 2.
a 2.
cresc. molto
cresc. molto
cresc. molto
cresc. molto
cresc. molto

a 2.
(ff)
a 2.
più cresc.
più cresc.
a 2.
più cresc.
a 2.
più cresc.
più cresc.
più cresc.
più cresc.
più cresc.
più cresc.
(Tb. ff)
mezzo piano
cresc.

I Maestoso assai (Andante). ♩=♩

Ohne Schlägel, die zwei Hülften der Becken schwingend gegeneinander geschlagen.
Without drumstick, the two halves of the cymbals clashed against each other.
Sans baguette, les deux disques des cymbales choqués l'un contre l'autre.

Orgel oder Harmonium.

Die Orgel (oder das Harmonium) im Hintergrund des Orchesters; bei Aufführungen im Theater, falls das Orchester nicht auf der Bühne, soll die Orgel hinter den Vorhang gestellt werden.
The Organ (or harmonium) to be in the rear of the orchestra, and when performed in a theatre, should the orchestra not be upon the stage, then the organ must be placed behind the curtain.
L'orgue (ou l'harmonium) doit être placé au fond de l'orchestre et dans les exécutions au théâtre, dans le cas où l'orchestre n'est pas sur la scène, derrière le rideau.

I Maestoso assai (Andante). ♩=♩

Lento.

a tempo

NB. Die Holzbläser tacent, wenn der Choral von dem Harmonium ausgeführt [wird].

The wood-instrument players observe Tacet, when the chorale is played by the harmonium.

Les joueurs d'instruments à vent en bois tiennent le tacet, si le choral est exécuté par l'harmonium.

In Ermanglung der Orgel (oder eines Harmoniums) übernehmen die Holzbläser den Choral.

Where no organ (or harmonium) is available, the wood-instrument players execute the chorale.

Faute d'orgue (ou d'harmonium) les joueurs d'instruments à vent en bois exécutent le choral.

Solo

dolce religioso

dolce religioso

dolce religioso

p dolce religioso

Lento.

a tempo

*) CHORAL:
Crux fidelis, inter omnes
Arbor una nobilis,
Nulla silva talem profert
Fronde, flore, germine
Dulce lignum, dulce clavos,
Dulce pondus sustinet.

Lento.

NB. Die Holzbläser tacent, wenn der Choral von dem Harmonium ausgeführt [wird].
The wood-wind players tacent if the chorale is taken by the harmonium.
Les joueurs d'instruments à vent en bois tiennent le tacet si le choral est exécuté par l'harmonium.

Solo.

Lento.

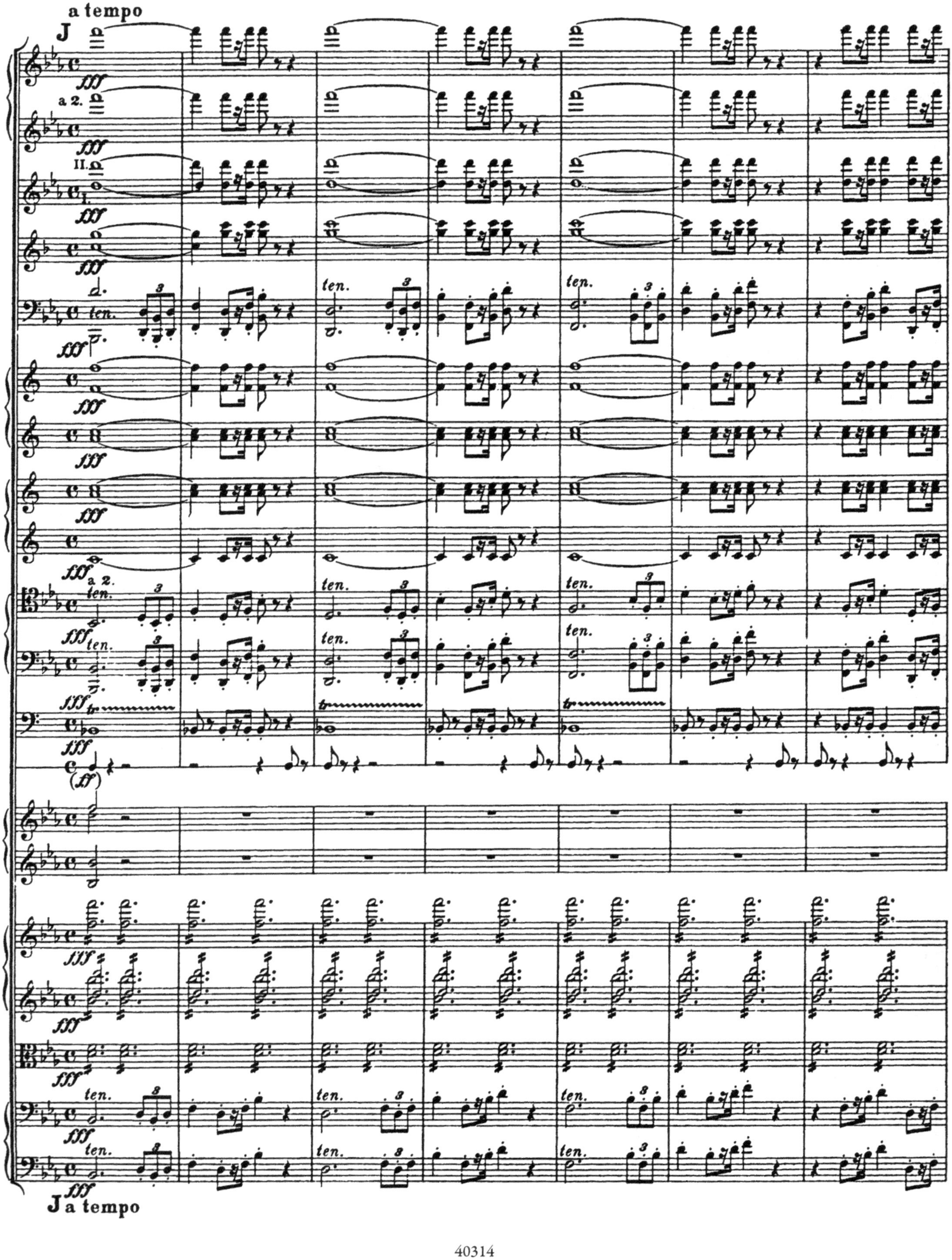
a tempo
J
a 2.
II.
I.
fff
ten.
tr
(ff)
J a tempo

62

K

Nicht schleppend, aber sehr ruhig.
Very quietly, without dragging.
Sans traîner, mais très tranquille.

Nicht schleppend, aber sehr ruhig.
Very quietly, without dragging.
Sans traîner, mais très tranquille.

40314

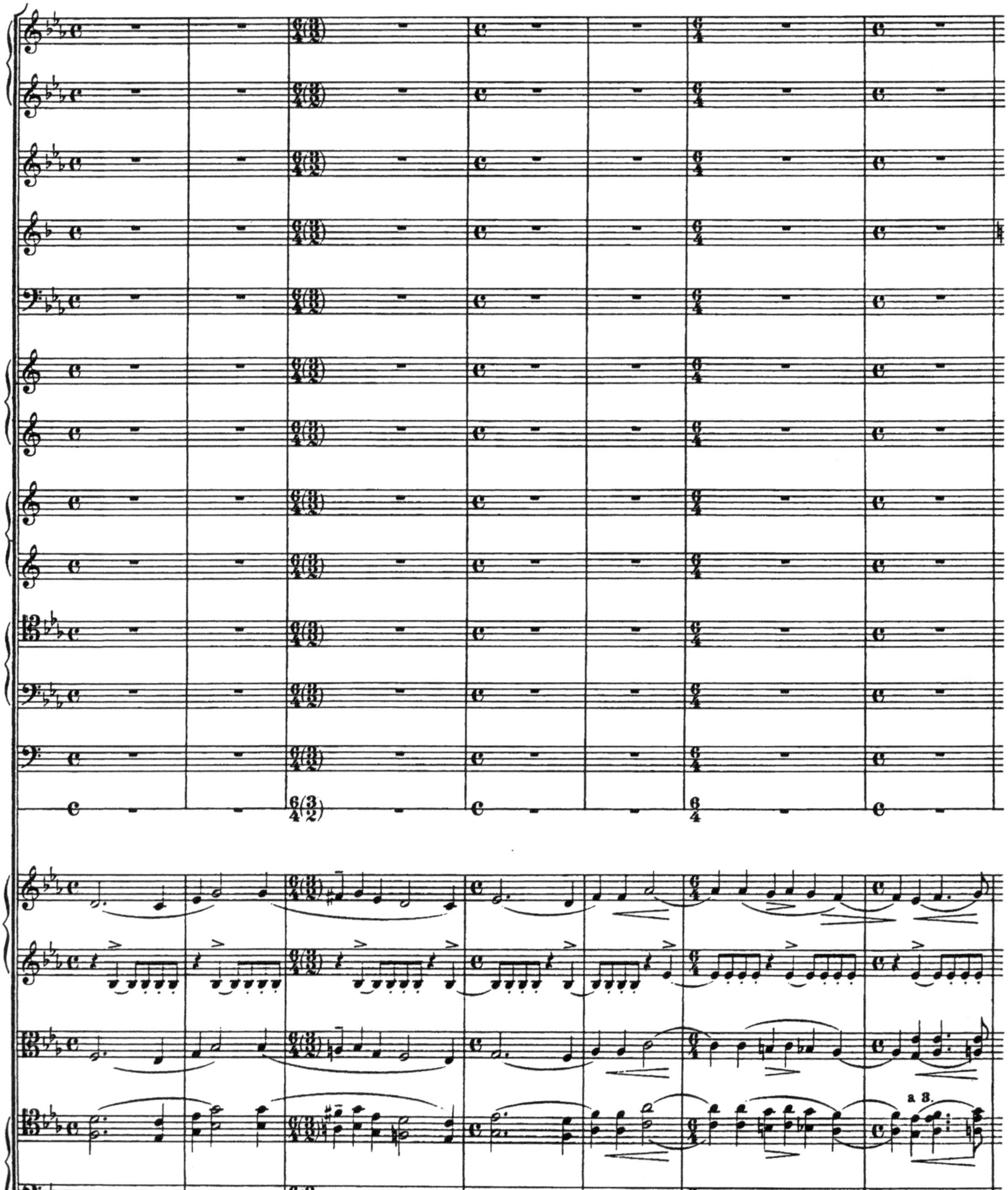
a 8.

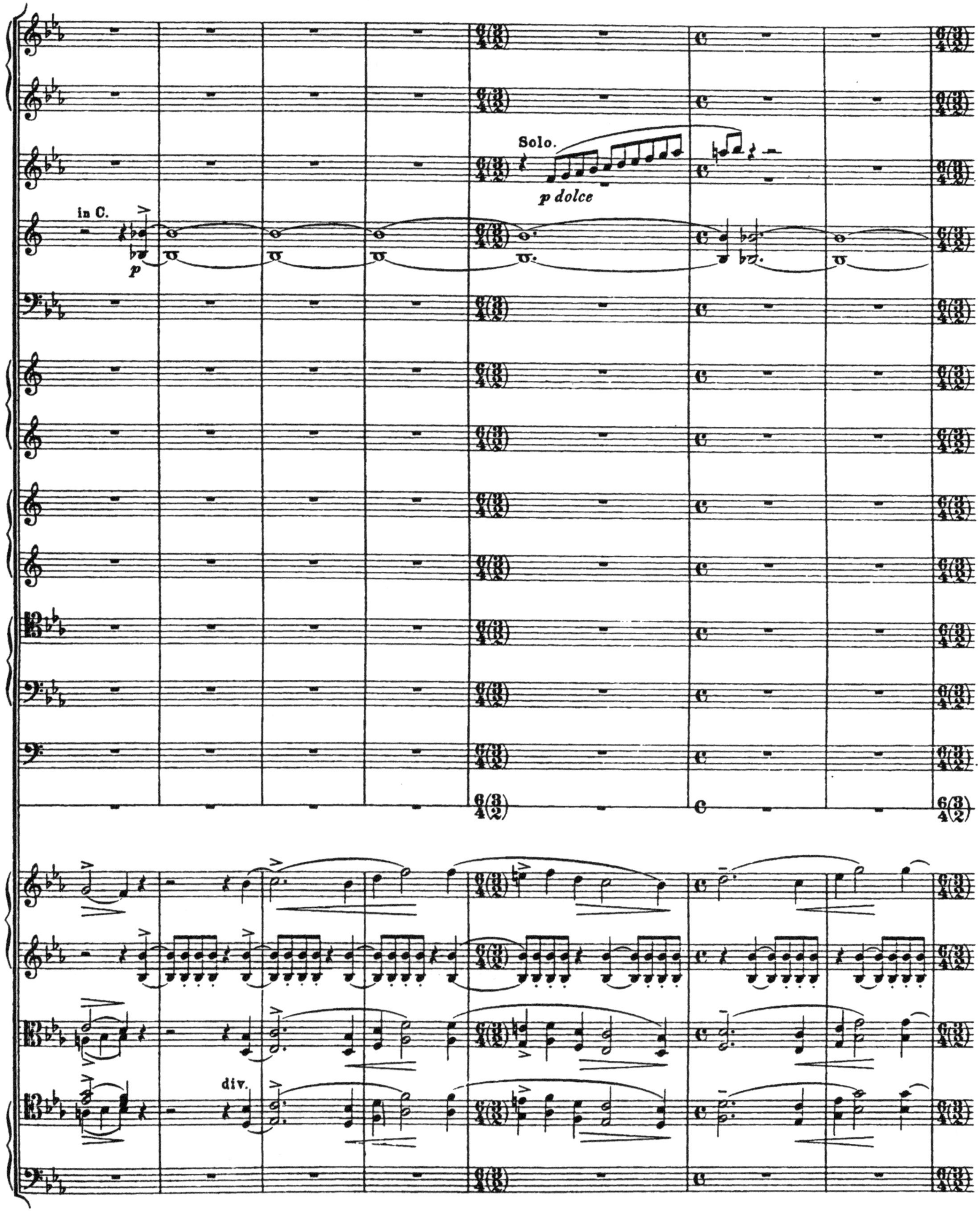
Solo.
p dolce
in C.
p
div.

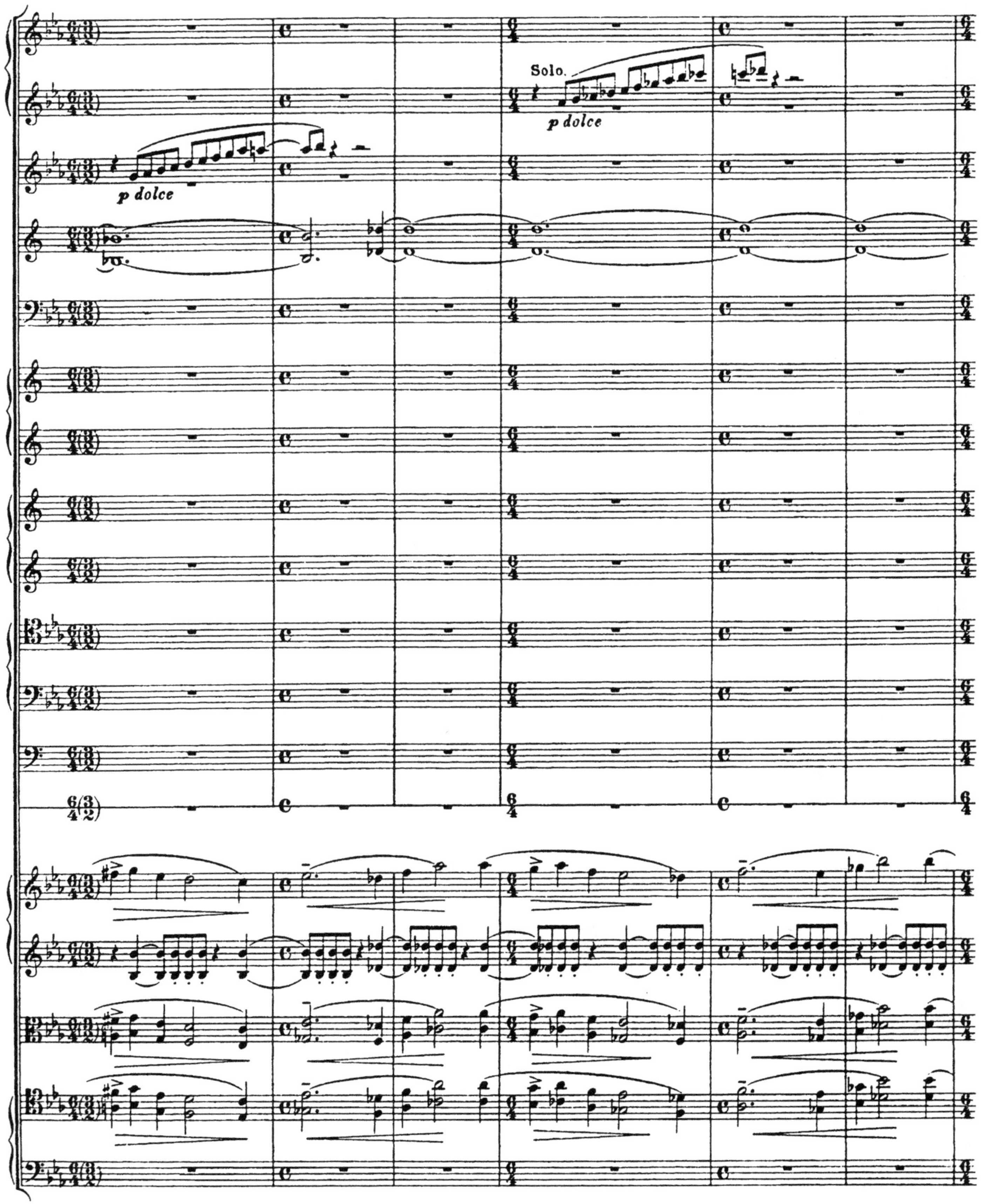
Solo.
p dolce
p dolce

L
sehr ruhig
molto tranquillo
dolciss.
sehr ruhig
molto tranquillo
dolciss.
Solo.
p
L

Der Buchstabe R.... bedeutet ein geringes Ritardando, so zu sagen: ein leises crescendo des Rhythmus.
The letter R.... signifies a slight Ritardando, so to speak: a gentle crescendo of the rhythm.
La lettre R.... signifie un petit Ritardando, c'est-à-dire: un doux crescendo du rhythme.

un poco rit.
M
Allegro. (Alla breve.)
perdendo
ppp
ppp
ppp
p cantabile
p
p
piano
M
Allegro. (Alla breve.)
un poco rit.

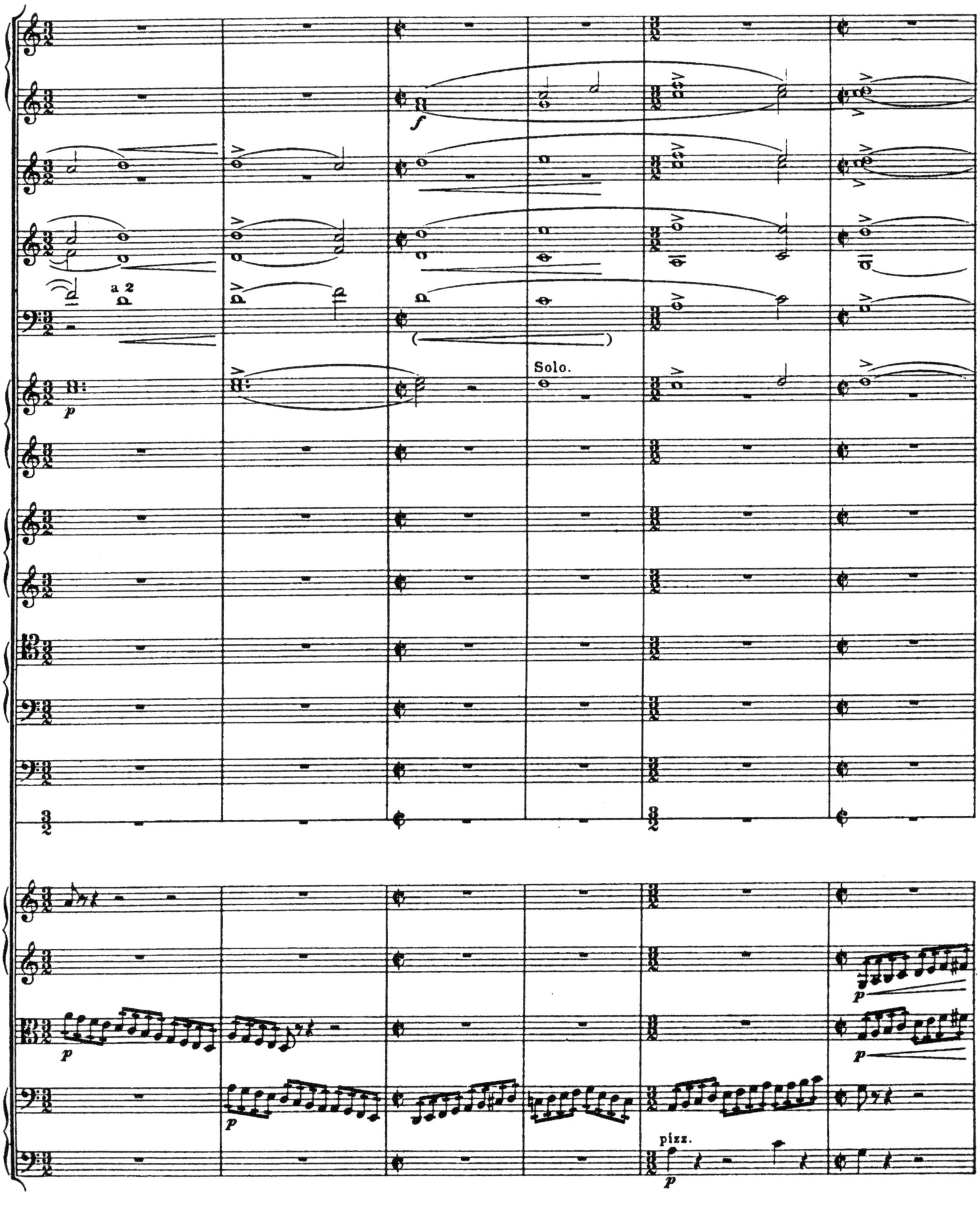
a 2
Solo.
pizz.

a 2.
(II. p)
Solo.
p
in C.
ten.
mf marc.
Solo.
mezzo f solenne
(II. mf)
ten.
in H. C. G.
mf
marc.
(p)
rinf.

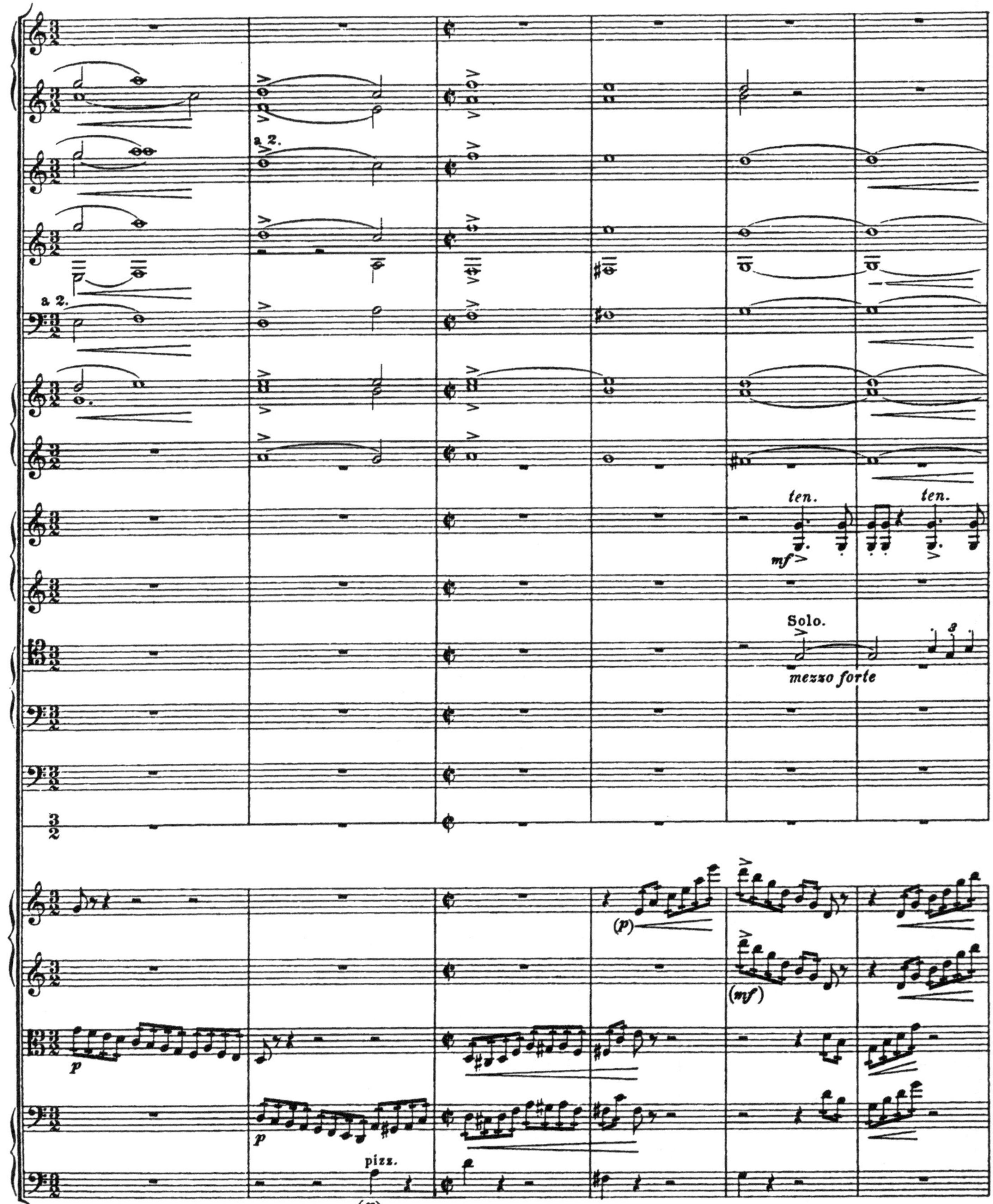
a 2.
a 2.
ten.
mf
ten.
Solo.
mezzo forte
(p)
(mf)
p
p
pizz.
(p)

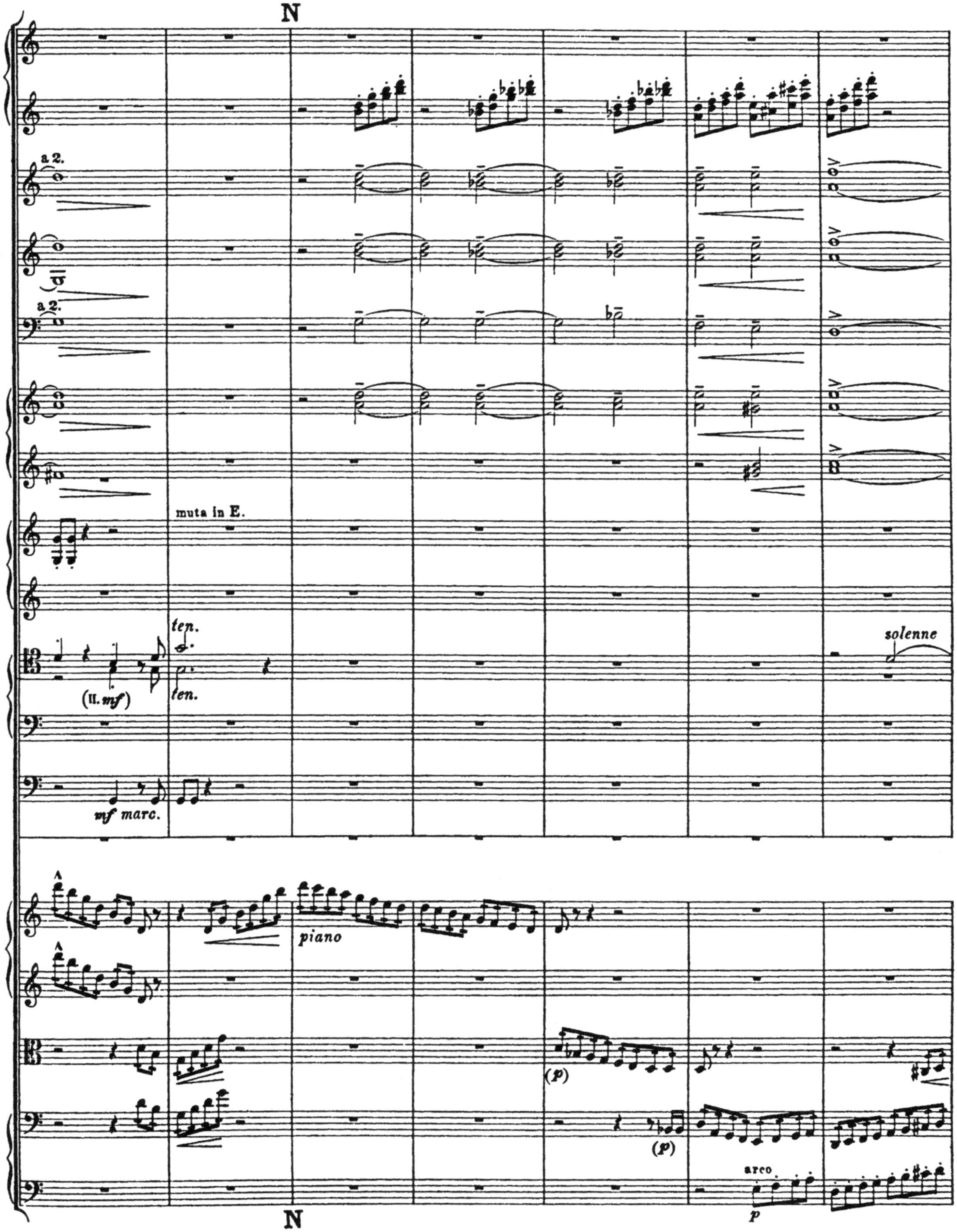
N
a 2.
a 2.
muta in E.
ten.
ten.
(II. mf)
solenne
mf marc.
piano
(p)
(p)
arco
p
N

74

40314

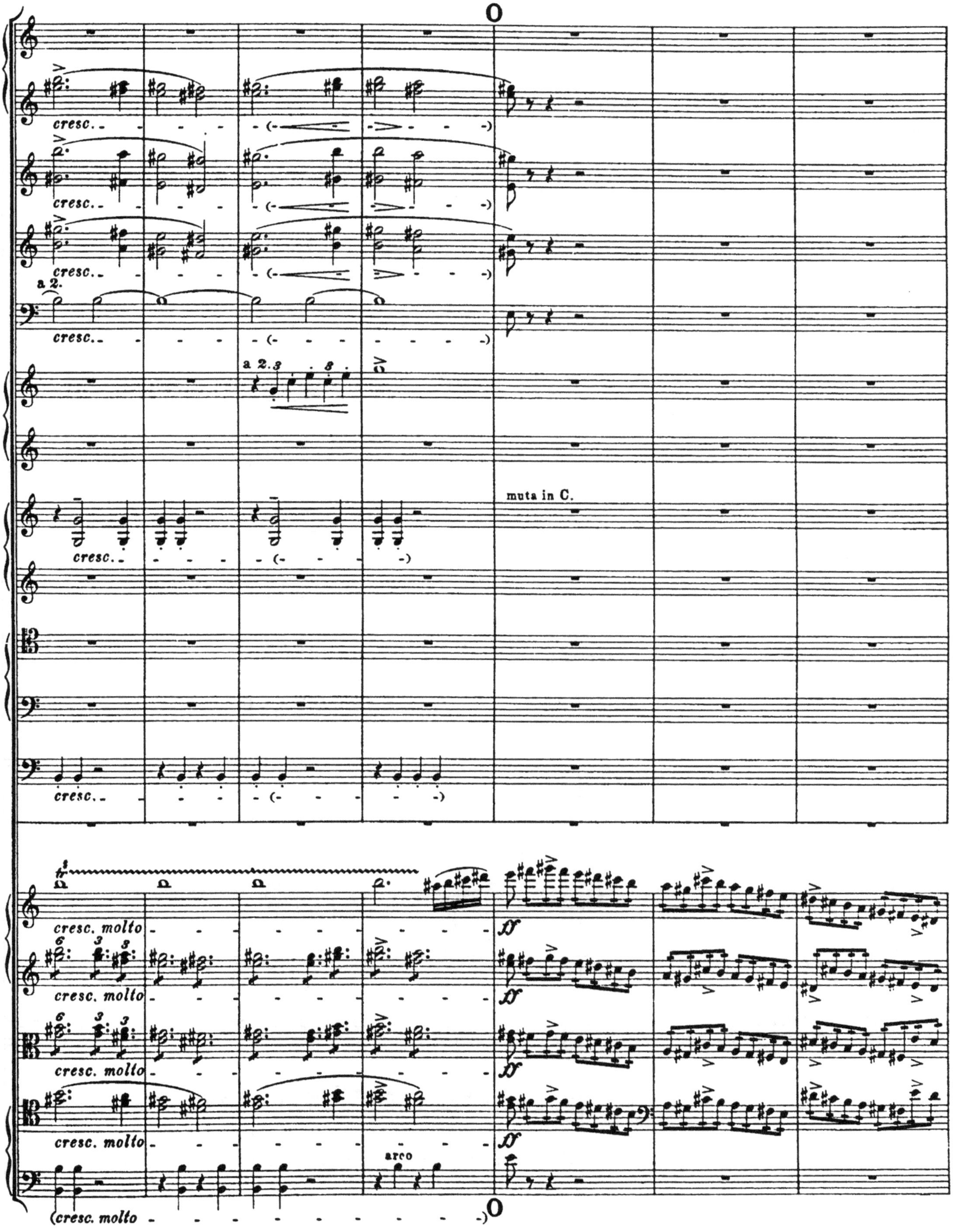
O
cresc.
a 2.
muta in C.
cresc. molto
arco
ff
(cresc. molto
O

Stretto.
a 2.
ff
p
a 2.
ff
p
a 2.
ff
muta in F.
in C.
a 2.
ff
p marc.
p
p
fp
dim.
p
fp
dim.
p
ff
Stretto.

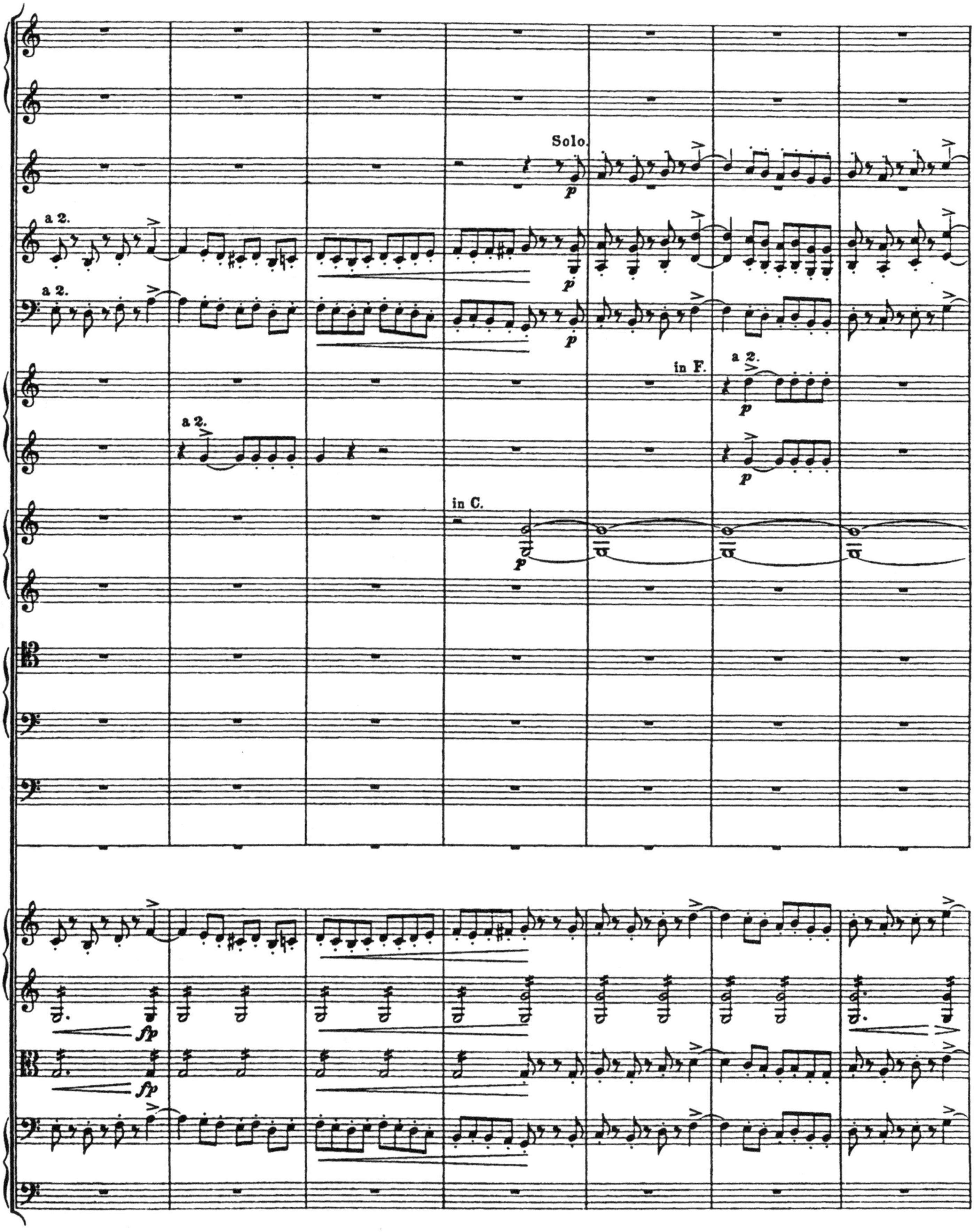
Solo.
p
a 2.
p
a 2.
p
in F.
a 2.
p
a 2.
p
in C.
p
fp
fp

P
a 2.
(f)
(mf)
(II. mf)
cresc.
a 2.
cresc.
a 2.
cresc.
a 2.
a 2.
cresc.
stacc. e cresc.
cresc.
(f)
sf
stacc. e cresc.
stacc. e cresc.
P
(mf) cresc.

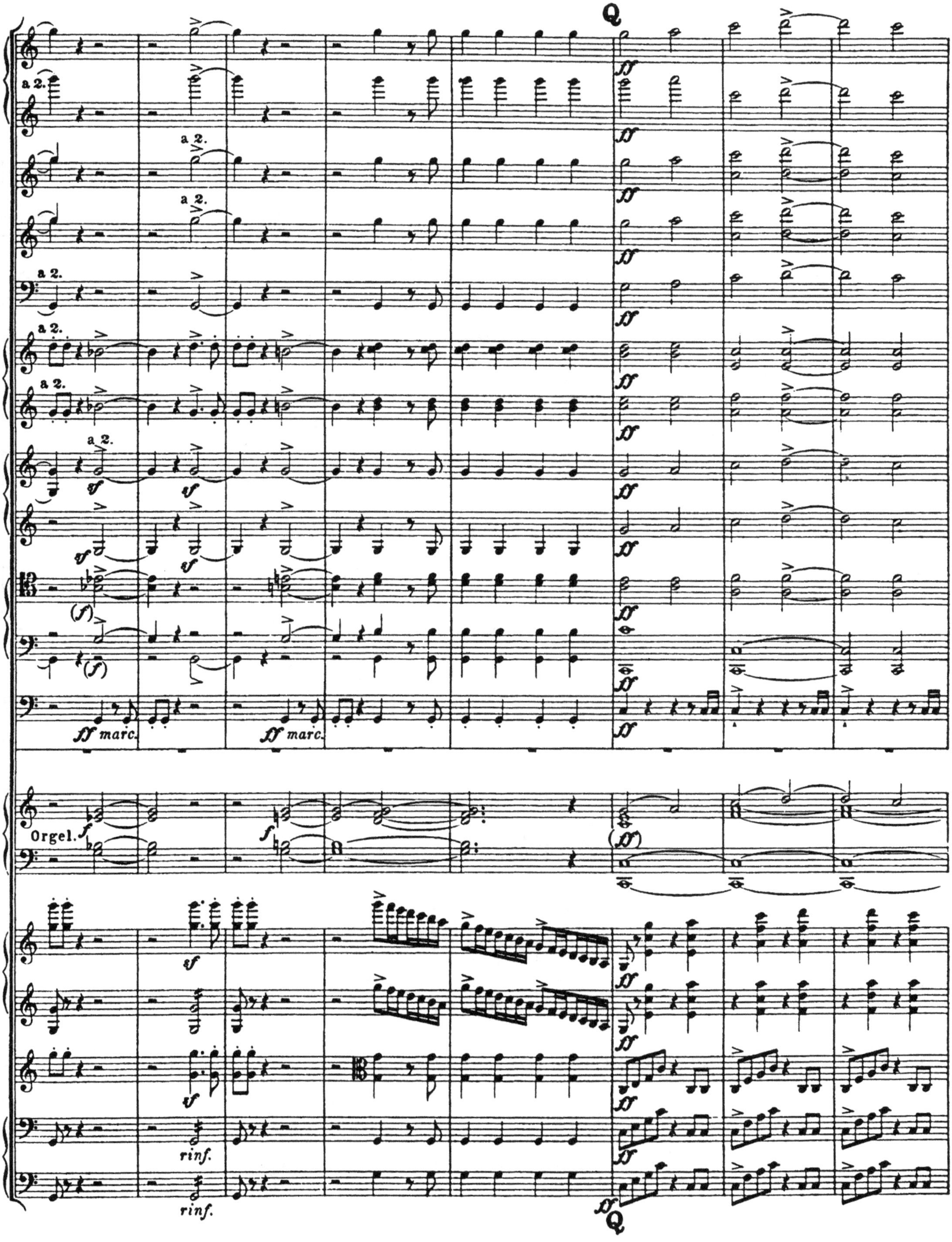
Q
a 2.
ff
sf
(f)
ff marc.
Orgel.
(ff)
rinf.
Q

den Rhythmus scharf hervorgehoben
the rhythm strongly accentuated
le rhythme très accentué

den Rhythmus scharf hervorgehoben
the rhythm strongly accentuated
le rhythme très accentué

ten.

fff pomposo

R
ff sempre
a 2.
ff sempre
ff sempre
ff sempre
a 2.
ff sempre
a 2.
ff sempre
a 2.
ff sempre
ff sempre
scharf
strongly accentuated
très accentué
ff sempre
ff sempre
ff sempre
scharf
strongly accentuated
très accentué
ff
ten.
fff pomposo
ten.
fff pomposo
ten.
fff pomposo
ten.
fff pomposo
ten.
R
fff pomposo

a 2.
a 2.
a 2.
a 2.
a 2.
ff scharf
strongly accentuated
très accentué
ff
ff
ff scharf
strongly accentuated
très accentué
ff
ff
fff
fff
fff
fff
fff
stacc.
stacc.
stacc.
stacc.
stacc.

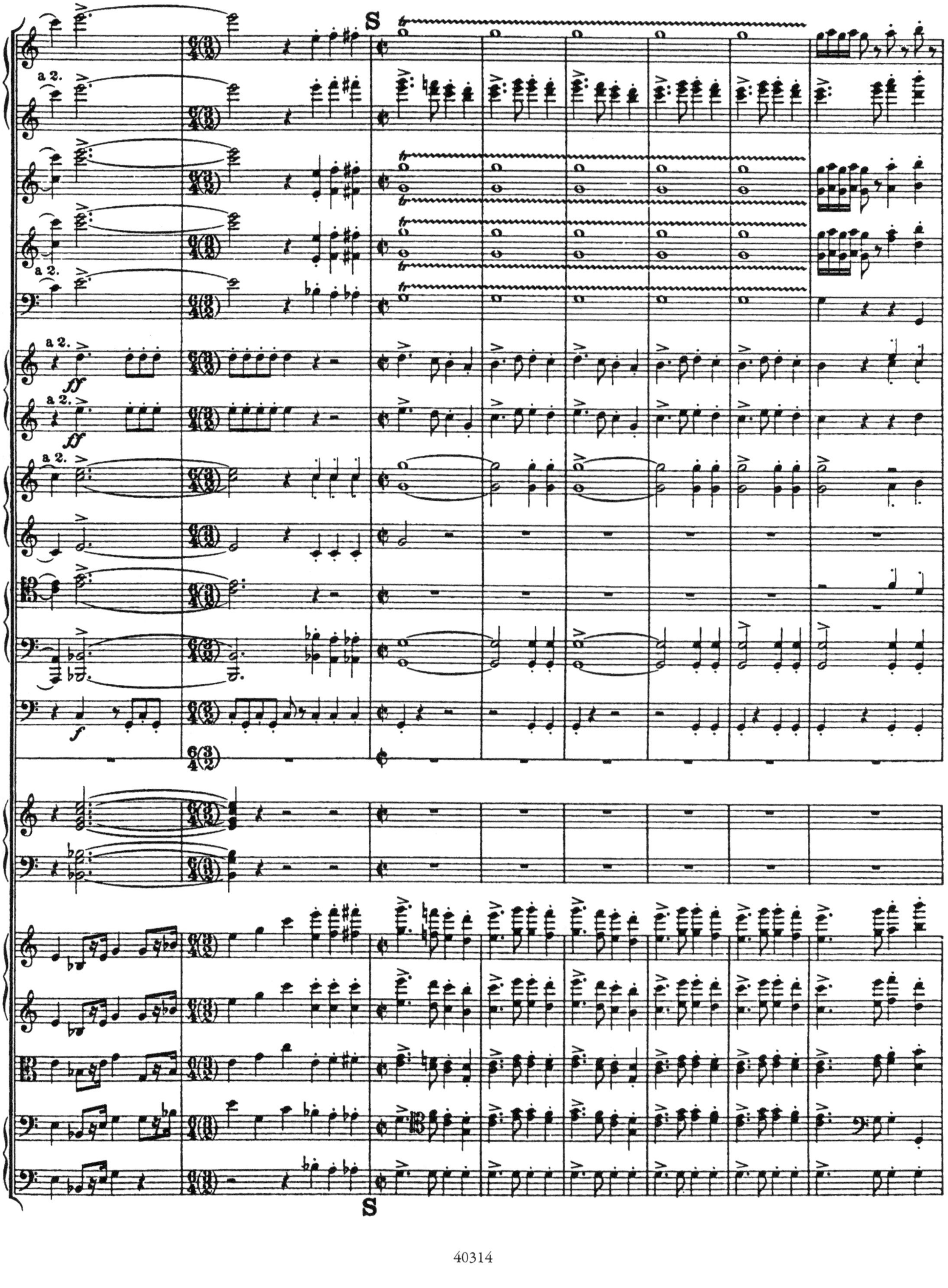
S
a 2.
ff
f
tr
S

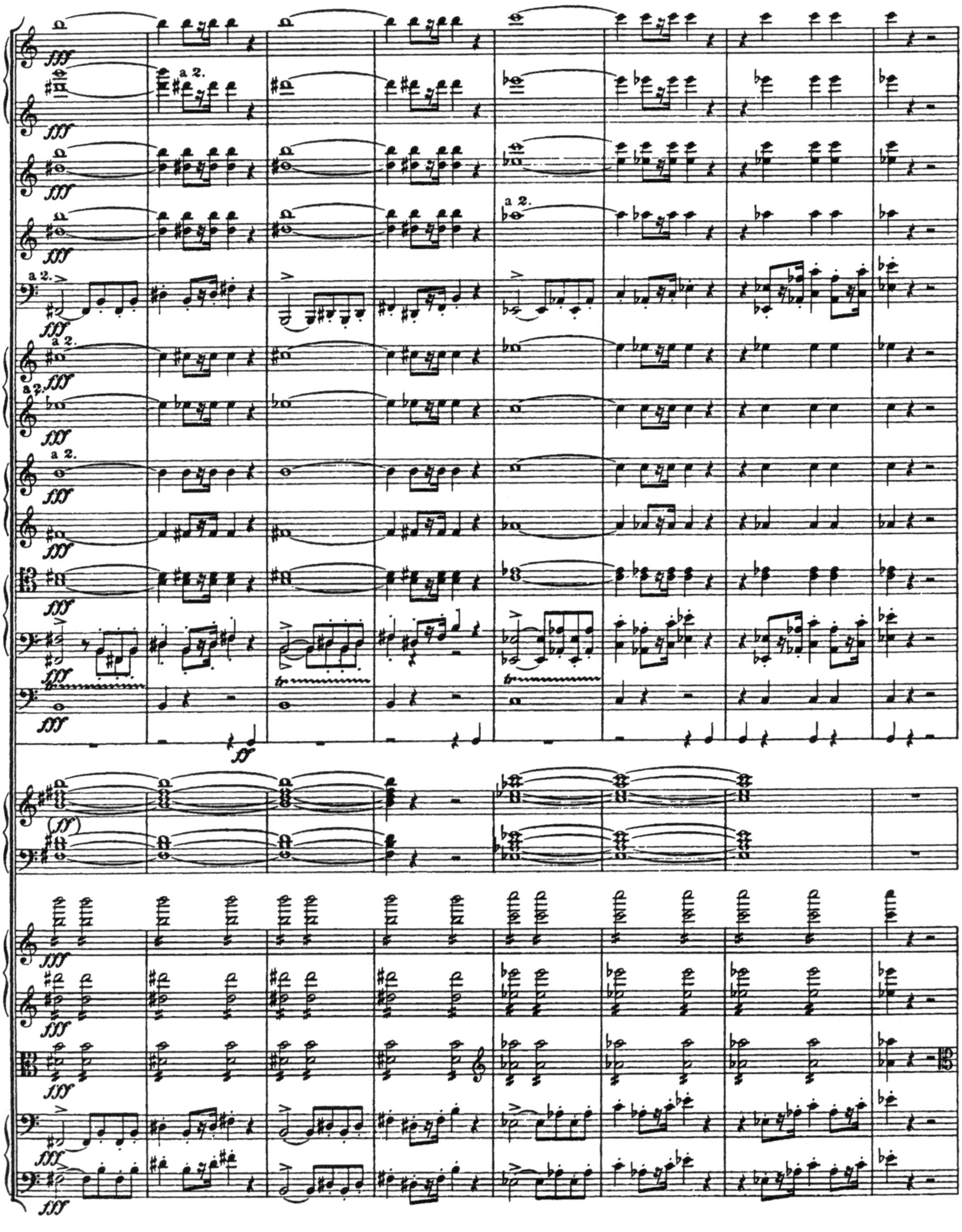
a 2.
a 2.
a 2.
a 2.
a 2.
a 2.
fff
tr
ff

*) Falls das Harmonium nicht genügend ausgiebig, um das Orchester am Schluss zu übertönen, soll es ganz wegbleiben.
If the harmonium is not strong enough to be heard above the Orchestra at the end, then it will be better to leave it out all together.
Dans le cas où l'harmonium ne serait pas assez puissant pour couvrir l'orchestre à la fin, n'en faire aucun usage.

Die Orgel sehr lange nachhallend.
The organ long sustained.
L'orgue très prolongé.

FRANZ LISZTS
SYMPHONISCHE DICHTUNGEN 11 u. 12

REVISIONSBERICHT

Im Jahre 1908 wurden in einer gemeinschaftlichen Sitzung der Revisoren, der Herausgeber und der Verleger die Leitgedanken und Grundsätze für eine vollständige, einheitliche und korrekte Gesamtausgabe der Werke Franz Liszts beraten und endgültig festgesetzt.

Aus praktischen Gründen der modernen Musikpflege mußten die vielfachen Unterschiede in der Benennung und Anordnung der Instrumente, in den Schlüsseln usw., vor allem aber sehr viele, für heutige Begriffe überflüssige oder selbst störende Versetzungszeichen beseitigt werden. Die auf letztere bezügliche Bestimmung lautet in endgültiger Fassung:

»Die von Liszt sehr reichlich angewendeten zufälligen Versetzungszeichen (namentlich Auflösungszeichen) sind für die heutige Praxis zum Teil entbehrlich geworden. Die nicht unbedingt notwendigen sind nur da beizubehalten, wo sie das Lesen tatsächlich noch erleichtern, Mißverständnisse verhüten oder für das harmonische Bild Lisztscher Schreibweise besonders charakteristisch erscheinen.«

Um jede Willkür auszuschliessen, sind alle irgendwie nennenswerten Änderungen, Weglassungen, Zusätze im Wortlaut der Lisztschen Partitur im Revisionsbericht je bei der betreffenden Komposition besonders aufgeführt und begründet worden, sodaß jeder mit der alten und der neuen Ausgabe in der Hand sich sein Urteil selbst bilden kann. Alle Zutaten, insbesondere Vortragsbezeichnungen, wurden in Klammern ( ) oder [ ] gesetzt; in einzelnen Fällen kann und soll dies nachträglich noch geschehen.

Die Herausgabe der Symphonischen Dichtungen war ursprünglich von Herrn Eugen d'Albert übernommen worden, der jedoch wegen anderweitiger großer Inanspruchnahme zurücktrat, nachdem er den Stich aller 12 Werke nur in erster Lesung hatte beaufsichtigen können. Die genaue Nachprüfung übernahm in dankenswerter Weise Herr Otto Taubmann in Berlin, in stetem Einvernehmen mit dem Kustos des Liszt-Museums, Herrn Hofrat Dr. Obrist, als dem Obmann der Revisionskommission.

BAND 6

HUNNENSCHLACHT.
Symphonische Dichtung Nr. 11.

Vorlage: Die erste Partiturausgabe, erschienen 1861 bei Breitkopf & Härtel in Leipzig. Verlagsnummer 10160.

Bemerkungen:

S. 18. Die Vorschrift der gedruckten Vorlage ›in 3 Viertel taktieren‹ wurde durch Weglassung des ›in‹ in ein korrektes Deutsch gebracht.

S. 18, 1. Takt — S. 19, 2. Takt. In der gedruckten Vorlage findet sich für die beiden ersten Hörner die ungebräuchliche Notierung

, die in die übliche geändert wurde.

S. 45, 1. Takt heißt es in den I. Violinen in der gedruckten Vorlage:

das Achtel c (dritte Note) ist, wie ein Vergleich mit Flöten und Hoboen, sowie mit der Parallelstelle auf S. 47, 2. Takt zeigt, ein Fehler; es muß ein Sechzehntel mit vorhergehender Sechzehntelpause sein.

S. 45, 3. Takt fehlt für 1. und 2. Horn in der gedruckten Vorlage die nach Analogie der Takte 2 und 4 auf S. 43 als nötig anzusehende Vorschrift ›gestopft‹.

S. 49. Während bei allen Streicherstellen, die ›mit breitem Strich‹ gespielt werden sollen, sonst jede Note die durchaus verständliche Bezeichnung ➤ hat, stehen in der gedruckten Vorlage über der I. und II. Violine im 4. und halben 5. Takt plötzlich Punkte. Auch die erste Stichvorlage hat Punkte, die von Liszt selbst ergänzt wurden. Aber er hat sicher nicht an die (übrigens auch erst vom Kopisten hinzugefügten) vorhergegangenen ➤ gedacht.

S. 55 hat die gedruckte Vorlage im 4. Takt für 3. und 4. Horn die augenscheinlich falsche Note (Klang b) statt des richtigen (Klang c); vergl. 2. Klar., 3. Tromp., 3. Posaune.

S. 61, 6. Takt wurde in der Orgel ein fehlender Bogen von as (¹/₂) zu as (¹/₄) in der Oberstimme ergänzt.

* * *

DIE IDEALE.
Symphonische Dichtung Nr. 12.

Vorlage: 1. Die erste Partiturausgabe, erschienen 1858 bei Breitkopf & Härtel. Verlagsnummer 9788.

2. Kürzungen, zusammen mit dem Anhang zu den Festklängen, 1861 erschienen. Verlagsnummer 10176.

Bemerkungen:

S. 21. Die Bezeichnung des Violoncell-Eintritts im 2. Takt mit der Angabe ›Solo‹ für die Oberstimme läßt es zweifelhaft erscheinen, ob nur ein Spieler die Oberstimme, oder ob die Hälfte aller Spieler sie ›mit solistischem Vortrage‹ wiedergeben soll. Vielleicht gibt die erste Stichvorlage einen Anhalt, in der sich von der Hand des Kopisten der Vermerk findet: { Solo / die übrigen Vclle.

S. 30. Die Bögen über den Triolen der Streicher stehen zum größten Teil nicht in der gedruckten Vorlage. Ihre Hinzufügung trotz der Vorschrift ›legatissimo sempre‹ wurde indessen nicht für überflüssig erachtet.

S. 42. Die gedruckte Vorlage hat im 4. Takt unter den ersten Violoncellen ein ◁ ▷, das ersichtlich zu den zweiten Violoncellen gehört. Der Fehler stammt aus einer Undeutlichkeit der ersten Stichvorlage, in der das ◁ ▷ dicht über den II. Violoncellen steht, was dann augenscheinlich falsch gedeutet wurde.

S. 46, 6. Takt steht in der gedruckten Vorlage für die I. Violine

. Das untere b ist als augenscheinlicher Stichfehler (siehe vorher und nachher) gestrichen worden.

S. 65, 2. Takt gilt für den Violoncell-Einsatz das über den gleichen Fall auf S. 21 Gesagte.

S. 72. Die sprachlich mangelhafte Vorschrift der gedruckten Vorlage ›im ³/₄ taktieren‹ wurde geändert in ›drei Schläge im Takt‹.

S. 79. Die sprachlich mangelhafte Vorschrift der gedruckten Vorlage ›im ²/₄ taktieren‹ wurde geändert in ›zwei Schläge im Takt‹.

S. 97. In der gedruckten Vorlage lautet der fünfte Takt in den Trompeten so:

Der Bogen von der Halben f zum c in der I. Trompete ist als Stichfehler entfernt worden; er steht auch nicht in der ersten Stichvorlage.

Eugen d'Albert Otto Taubmann
Berlin. Berlin.

Dr. Aloys Obrist
Weimar.